JOURNEY TO ETHIOPIA

1962 – 1964

NYLE KARDATZKE

OTHER BOOKS BY NYLE KARDATZKE

Widow-man: A Widower's Story and Journaling Book, 2014
The Brown House Stories: A Child's Garden of Eden, 2015
The Clock of the Covenant, 2016
The Summertime of Our Lives: Stories from a Marriage, 2019
Leatherport, Ohio: Stories from the Great Black Swamp, 2021
Dacoma, Oklahoma, USA: Stories from the West, 2022

Copyrighted Material

Journey to Ethiopia: 1962-1964

Copyright © 2025 by Nyle Kardatzke

All Rights Reserved. No part of this publication may be reproduced, stored in a retrieval system or transmitted, in any form or by any means—electronic, mechanical, photocopying, recording or otherwise—without prior written permission from the publisher, except for the inclusion of brief quotations in a review.

All Scripture quotations, unless otherwise indicated, are taken from the Holy Bible, New International Version®, NIV®. Copyright ©1973, 1978, 1984, 2011 by Biblica, Inc.™ Used by permission of Zondervan. All rights reserved worldwide. www.zondervan.com The "NIV" and "New International Version" are trademarks registered in the United States Patent and Trademark Office by Biblica, Inc.™

New Fabrika. Glass tea cup isolated on white background. Digital Image. Shutterstock. Web. 22 November 2024.

Ethio Kapture. An Ethiopian traditionally brewed cup of Arabica coffee. Digital Image. Shutterstock. Web. 22 November 2024.

Peyker. Vintage spindle in thread isolated on white background. Digital Image. Shutterstock. Web. 22 November 2024.

Elena Ska. Man wearing traditional cloths in Ethiopian Highlands near Lalibela. Digital Image. Shutterstock. Web. 22 November 2024.

Fizzl. The bar counter of African cafe with many traditional Ethiopian jebena boiling pots for brewing the coffee for the coffee ceremony. Digital Image. Shutterstock. Web. 10 December 2024.

Map drawn by Anna Herman

For information about this title contact the author:
Nyle Kardatzke
Email: nylebk@gmail.com

ISBN: 978-1-7328222-9-0 (softcover)
       978-1-7328222-8-3 (ebook)

Printed in the United States of America
Cover and Interior design and Editorial Services: 1106 Design

DEDICATION

THIS BOOK IS DEDICATED to Ethiopians whose friendship contributed so much to my two years in their country. Those friends include Isaac Joseph, my closest Ethiopian friend; our Headmaster, Iob Aria; our cook and housekeeper Lete Dehab Habut; and Umberto Bosi and Fetui Ghebrejohannes, who assisted Lete at different times.

Like other Peace Corps teachers, I am indebted to the students who struggled to understand our version of English. I'm also indebted to the students who tutored us on many aspects of Ethiopian culture. Among the students were Aregai Tecle, Yemane Russom, Tsehainesh Ghebrejohannes, Haile Ghebremusie, and Tzeggai Woldat. I regret that the names of other students have escaped me after all these years.

This book also owes its existence to several Americans. The experiences it describes could not have happened without the visionary leadership of the late American President John Fitzgerald Kennedy; the first Peace Corps Director, Sargent Shriver; and Harris Wofford, the first national director of the Peace Corps in Ethiopia. Bill Canby provided leadership and wisdom as the director for the sixty Peace Corps Volunteers who served in Eritrea when I was there.

Many of the experiences described in the book were shared with the other Peace Corps Volunteers in Adi Ugri. Those volunteers were Gloria

JOURNEY TO ETHIOPIA: 1962-1964

Somple Perrino, who taught in Adi Ugri for two years, as did I. The other Volunteers in 1962-63 were Jackie Woodson, Cynthia Tse (Kimberlin), and Bill Kerske. In the 1963-64 year, Jody Donovan, Katie Schulz, and John Rude joined Gloria Perrino and me to teach at the St. George School.

TABLE OF CONTENTS

Acknowledgements ix

Author's Introduction xi

Prologue xiii

Map of Eritrea and Ethiopia xiv

Chapter 1: In the Quiet Waters of the Midwest 1

Chapter 2: The Invitation 9

Chapter 3: Preparations 13

Chapter 4: Departures and Arrivals 27

Chapter 5: To Eritrea in the North 39

Chapter 6: Adi Ugri 47

Chapter 7: St. George School 61

Chapter 8: Traveling Tales 81

Chapter 9: Adi Gaba with the Missionaries 91

Chapter 10: History Lessons 107

Chapter 11: Christmas 1962 111

Chapter 12: Summer 1963 in the Middle East 125

Chapter 13: Teaching Tales 139

Chapter 14: Kenya and Uganda Travel 1964 155

Chapter 15: Student Stories 161

Appendix: Roads and Villages of Eritrea 183

ACKNOWLEDGEMENTS

I AM GRATEFUL TO RONDA Rawlins, and Kayla Cook who patiently answered my questions and guided me through the editing process.

My daughter, Jenny Rasmussen and her family were the inspiration for actually getting these experiences into book form by their interest and engagement as I shared some of these stories with them one evening.

My daughter, Anna Herman came alongside me during the editing process and helped put the finishing touches on the book.

My son, Matt Kardatzke was instrumental in locating all of the pictures used in the book.

My daughter-in-law, Kathryn Kardatzke helped with logistics of printing and mailing various drafts back and forth to Anna.

I am grateful also to my editor, the late Karen Roberts, who advised me in the early stages of the writing of this book.

AUTHOR'S INTRODUCTION

I WENT TO ETHIOPIA IN 1962 AS A MEMBER of the Peace Corps. When I left Ethiopia in 1964, I was a changed young man but I didn't realize how deeply I had been affected by my time in that ancient, modernizing land.

I was young and had no training in anthropology or sociology, so during my two-year stay I could make only naïve observations of what appeared before my wondering eyes. I lived in a small city named Adi Ugri, and I fell in love with the place. I wish I could return to the town as it was in 1962, but progress has won over sentiment; the world has changed.

I kept only a thin diary in Ethiopia, so this book is based mainly on my memories.

The angle of the sun, in the semi-desert, and the thin mountain air were pleasant and stimulating. Daily living was sometimes like a journey into Bible times: camels trudged into town with their burdens; herds of sheep, goats, and cattle were driven to the weekly market; and three faiths contended openly for the hearts of the people. The Tigrinya language at first sounded harsh, with unpronounceable consonants and vowels that came from deep in the throat. The taste of hot Ethiopian food held all those indelible memories together.

The book is as accurate as I can make it. You may read it as a myth or some other form of writing, but it is factual. Where possible, I have checked my memories through the modern mysteries of life such as Google, Google Maps, and Wikipedia. I hope what you read here will increase your interest in the foreigners living near you here in America. If you meet any Eritreans, they may be surprised when you tell them you know a little about their country. If you spend time with them, you can learn about their country without leaving home.

From 1962 to 1964, my complete mailing address was "Nyle Kardatzke, Adi Ugri, Eritrea, Ethiopia." My name, "Nyle Kardatzke," is so unusual that it sometimes leads me to explain it by saying, "It sounds like the river." People often don't understand, because they haven't heard of a "Kardatzke River," and they don't immediately think of the Nile River. It must have been providential that I spent two years in Ethiopia and in my travels saw the sources of both the Blue Nile and the White Nile and long stretches of the Nile River in Egypt.

PROLOGUE

MANY FORMER PEACE CORPS VOLUNTEERS have written books and essays about their experiences around the world, so there seemed to be no need for another Peace Corps book until I took one of my daughters and her family to an Ethiopian restaurant in Indianapolis. The dinner included traditional Ethiopian dishes, and even the young children helped us eat trays of meat, vegetables, and the rubbery Ethiopian bread called *injera*.

At my home that night, we started a fire in the fireplace, and I began telling my family about the pictures of Ethiopia that hung on a wall near the fireplace. They were excited by the stories and kept listening until late that night.

The next morning, I took my daughter and her family to the airport for their flight home to Houston. That same day, I started a memory dump on my computer. I wrote memories as they came to my mind and numbered them just to know how many memories there were. That list of reminders kept growing while I wrote other books. Over time, I recorded over six hundred memories. Some memories were single words or phrases, and other memories would become whole chapters. Now, in the book's final form, these combined memories paint a picture of a time and place more amazing now than they seemed sixty years ago.

JOURNEY TO ETHIOPIA: 1962-1964

ERITREA AND ETHIOPIA

CHAPTER 1

IN THE QUIET WATERS OF THE MIDWEST

How it all Began

EVERY RIVER STARTS SOMEWHERE, even if the source is sometimes hard to find. The Blue Nile River, for example, starts as a tiny stream on the west side of Lake Tana in northern Ethiopia. The river flows into Lake Tana and its path through the lake can be traced to the south end of the lake. From there it flows south to the roaring Tis Abay or Blue Nile Falls. From there the river loops to the east and takes a wide, swooping course west into the Sudan. It meets the White Nile River at Khartoum to form the Nile River that waters and nourishes Egypt before the river empties into the Mediterranean Sea.

My life in Ethiopia began in the American Midwest, in Ohio and Indiana through 35-mm slide shows brought to our church by missionaries who had worked in Kenya. For me as a young boy, the most interesting pictures were sensational, showing women with gigantically swollen necks where their thyroid glands were swollen into goiters. In other pictures, women's

JOURNEY TO ETHIOPIA: 1962-1964

legs were so swollen they imitated those of elephants, the result of a disease called elephantiasis caused by worms carried by mosquitoes. The spiritual point of the missionary talks was mostly lost on my pagan young mind, but I was drawn to the sights of exotic, faraway places. Strange new foods and diseases appealed to my childish sensuality. The seeds were planted, but I never imagined I would ever go to the places where the missionaries had been.

Kenya became a family matter when my Uncle Carl and Aunt "Tip" Kardatzke spent two years there working in mission schools. The danger they faced during the Mau Mau uprising made their time in Kenya seem like something from an adventure movie. Carl's experiences led his youngest brother, my Uncle Elmer Kardatzke, and his wife, Vera, to visit Kenya. They brought back stories of elephants and of a food called *obasuma* (soft balls of cornmeal). Elmer and Vera brought gifts to all of the kids in my family, and my gift was a leather coin purse from Egypt with a picture of the pyramids stamped onto the cover. I could almost see Joseph on that coin purse, but I never expected to see the pyramids in person.

In a college psychology class, I learned that entering a different culture can raise your IQ, or Intelligence Quotient, evidently by stimulating your mind more than your home culture could. Seeking a higher IQ had nothing to do with my entering the Peace Corps, but later, when I saw what a turning point my two years in Ethiopia had been, I could see that it had been a great awakening for me and had perhaps made me a little more intelligent.

I was led into the Peace Corps as if by an "invisible hand" to quote Adam Smith in his famed book *The Wealth of Nations*.

First, I "accidentally" entered Anderson College (Anderson, Indiana) in 1957 through the influence of my Uncle Carl. He had been the first of our family name to graduate from high school and was the first to go to college. He was Vice President of the College in 1957 and had influenced several of my cousins to enroll at the college. Their presence at Anderson College led me to start there as a freshman in 1957. Carl died in January 1959 of liver cancer, and there was deep, widespread grief because of his far-reaching ministry on marriage and family life as well as his memorable college teaching.

In spring 1959, I joined the Triad social club, and a few weeks later the club members asked me to be their nominee for Vice President of the Student Council. I had been working off campus, and I hadn't been in any campus activities. I had no record to run on, so name recognition must have caused me to win over the other four candidates for the office of Student Council Vice President.

The Student Council President that year was Carol Harting, a young woman who was studying history and political science and knew how to act as a student politician. She was a successful President, and her glory shone on me. I was elected President in 1960, partly as a tribute to her.

I had become a math major, a subject the Peace Corps, though it didn't yet exist, would need. Math alone might not have gotten me into the Peace Corps, but my college political career may have seemed to guarantee publicity for them. That potential publicity plus my math major evidently did the trick.

First Steps toward the Peace Corps

My first steps toward the Peace Corps happened quietly in my mind. Part of my awakening was John F. Kennedy's election in 1960. He projected a vision for America that seemed to offer purpose and excitement to young people like me. His vision of a "New Frontier" appealed to my sense of history and my family's own history on the American frontier. In his campaign, Kennedy announced that he would create a program to send young Americans with needed skills to Third World countries. He also wanted young Americans to gain a better understanding of cultures different from ours. He didn't use the name "Peace Corps" in his first speech about it, but that name came soon. Serving in the Peace Corps seemed to me like an impossible dream, but if I could get in, I might be able to go to Africa as a penniless young man. I might even do some good.

Kennedy's Peace Corps announcement reminded me of two books I had read. *The Ugly American* (1958) by William J. Lederer and Eugene Burdick told how Americans often stumbled in their work in a fictional low-income country because they were ignorant of the language and culture. *A Nation of Sheep* (1961) by Lederer was a call for a more ambitious version of America than the TV culture that had sprung up in the 1950s. Both books were critical of some Americans' behavior overseas. The timidity and lack of direction described in *A Nation of Sheep* made me want to do something about America's role in the world. The Peace Corps seemed a way for me to offer practical help in Third World nations. "Third World" meant that they were not aligned with America or Russia in the Cold War.

My family had made nearly annual trips from Ohio to Oklahoma to visit relatives there. One of our more distant trips even took us to Tijuana, Mexico. I began to realize that other countries could be very different from mine. At my young age, I especially liked the colorful trinkets I could buy cheaply in Mexico; my interests were shallow.

In college, studying French broadened my view of the world. I knew nothing of France except the stories and pictures in my French textbook, but I felt something pulling me to go there if I ever had the chance.

My ambition for foreign travel and righting the wrongs of the world remained hardly more than a daydream until I began to notice politics in 1960, especially John F. Kennedy's candidacy. I was in the crowd on the day Kennedy gave a campaign speech in downtown Anderson, Indiana in October 1960.

Kennedy was campaigning in the Midwest and had scheduled a stop in Anderson, a heavily Democratic town. I was one of the Anderson College students who walked to the 1870s brick courthouse in downtown Anderson. His caravan of cars was delayed by a bank robbery along his route from Indianapolis, so we waited more than an hour to see him. I don't remember a word he said that day. All I remember is pigeons circling the courthouse ominously. They were like a scene in the 1959 movie "On the Beach," in which a nuclear war had released radiation that was killing all humans and all other life on earth. If Kennedy were to win the election, I knew that he could lead the country into a nuclear war like the one in the movie. The fluttering pigeons at the courthouse gave the day a heavy feel.

The election of 1960 was very close, and Kennedy edged out Richard Nixon with help from heavy voting in Chicago and a few other places. He won the popular vote by only 113,000 votes out of the 68 million that had been cast, but Kennedy won 303 to 219 in the electoral college. Richard Nixon declined to challenge the election outcome, saying, "I wouldn't want the election on those terms," but his Republican Party lodged complaints in eleven states. "The rest," as they say, "is history."

Kennedy's inauguration in January 1961 was something other students at Anderson College watched on TV while I was busy with a Student Council project. The inauguration seemed a dull government function, so I didn't watch it. I learned later that the podium had smoldered dangerously when Cardinal Richard Cushing delivered the invocation prayer. Poet Robert Frost was unable to see to read the poem he had composed for the occasion, but he received a roaring ovation when he recited it from memory.

Kennedy had proposed something like the Peace Corps at a campaign rally at the University of Michigan in fall 1960. Soon after his inauguration, Kennedy's first action on the Peace Corps was an executive order launching it, and it was later formally adopted by an act of Congress.

The Peace Corps soon began to make news. The first Peace Corps volunteers entered training in 1961, and soon a Peace Corps girl in Ghana wrote a postcard about the conditions in that country. Someone in the Ghana post office showed the card to a news reporter, and the postcard was soon world news. The postcard incident was a huge embarrassment to the United States, but it gave the Peace Corps more publicity than the quiet work of other young volunteers who were already at work in several countries.

In its early days, the Peace Corps was sometimes described as "the moral equivalent of war," an allusion to a speech (1906) and an essay (1910) titled "The Moral Equivalent of War" by the philosopher William James. He wrote of the need to sustain political unity and civic virtue without war, and he called for service in the interests of both the individual and the nation. I hadn't heard the speech, nor had I read the essay, but the Peace Corps idea of attacking poverty and ignorance in something like warfare appealed to my young mind.

In fall 1961, I attended a weekend conference for prospective theology students at Oberlin College in Ohio. Most of the speakers were pastors of large churches, and they spoke of budgets and financial issues and problems managing committees and volunteers. One pastor was different. He was a tall, lanky guy who looked as though he might have tied up his horse just outside the building. He explained that he was a circuit rider with a car, pastoring three tiny churches in rural Southern Ohio. He said the problem in his churches was not organizational or financial issues. The problem in his churches was *sin*, he said, waving an arm in the air and nearly shouting. The lives of his congregants were damaged by the same wayward desires the Bible denounced, and he preached a gospel of repentance, like the message of John the Baptist. His desire to get to the root of things outside formal organizational structures inspired me with a glimpse of what I vaguely hoped to find in my future.

A month later, I went to Chicago with the Anderson College Dean of Students for a one-day conference that explained and promoted the Peace Corps. I remember almost nothing about the conference except that its purpose was to help college administrators explain the Peace Corps to prospective volunteers. My clearest memory of the conference was a brief opening greeting from Chicago's Mayor Richard Daly. He probably said he hoped we would have a good time in Chicago, and he probably hoped we would spend some money there. I never saw him again in person, but I saw him on TV in 1968 when demonstrators tried to disrupt the Democratic National Convention in Chicago. (Mayor Daley was not a happy man that day, and he didn't ask the demonstrators to have a good time.)

The Chicago conference led me to fill out an application for the Peace Corps. The internet and email had not been invented, so I sent a letter to the Peace Corps asking for an application. I completed the paper application with a ballpoint pen, something unheard of now in the times of online applications. The application asked my preferred place of service, and I wrote "Kenya," the only foreign place I knew about because of missionaries who had spoken at our church in Ohio.

I had read that the Peace Corps was receiving thousands of applications, and the acceptance rate was low. Graduating from a small Midwestern Christian college didn't seem to put me on the inside track to the Peace Corps, but at least my name was in the hopper.

I also applied for Navy Officer Candidate School, and in March 1962 I received an invitation to enter training and join the Navy. The Navy required that I make a four-year commitment after six to seventeen weeks in training, depending on the specialty the Navy would choose for me. I gulped at the thought of being in the Navy or *anywhere* for four years. That would have been nearly a fifth of my life at that time.

The Navy had its appeal. As a Navy officer I would have a fancy uniform with brass buttons. Maybe I would be on a very big ship and sail all over the world, keeping the world peaceful. I would be called "sir," and I would call everyone else "sir"—but just the men. But then I read the fine print on the invitation. It said I was to be a "supply officer." This meant that the Navy thought I was good with numbers because of my math major, and I might be trainable as an accountant. I pictured myself in a huge warehouse overseeing storage of everything from uniforms to heavy weapons. My warehouse might be in Georgia, and there probably would be no air conditioning.

While pondering my future warehouse position one afternoon, I came upon the Dean of Students, Norman Beard, in the lobby of Anderson College's Old Main building. I told him about the offer and my reluctance to spend four years in a Georgia warehouse. He thought a moment and said, "I've never thought of the military as being a very creative place to work. It's necessary and good, but it's pretty confining."

His words spoke to my deepest concerns about my Navy career. I probably would have a nice uniform, but I wouldn't be on an aircraft carrier or on a submarine. I would only sail away in a big, hot warehouse in Georgia or someplace like it. Before the time limit expired, I turned down the Navy offer, and I had no future plans.

Near the end of each school year, Anderson College had a Senior Chapel honoring and bidding farewell to the graduating class. I was a former student politician, and I was asked to give a speech. In my speech, I told of a dream I had had in which I was walking in the halls of Old Main, opening door after door looking for my purpose in life. In the dream, I didn't find my purpose, but I kept looking, and in my speech, I encouraged the students to open new doors until they found a room to enter, a place where they could fulfill their purpose.

The other speaker that day was Ruben Schweiger, son of Kenya missionaries. In January 1964, Ruben and his wife, Ginny, showed me around Nairobi when I visited him on a trip from Ethiopia. When we gave our speeches in Indiana in 1962, neither of us imagined meeting in Kenya less than two years later.

In spring 1962, I was a student teacher in Lapel, Indiana, I was enjoying teaching ninth grade algebra, the one math subject I was competent to teach. I had nearly forgotten my Peace Corps application and had begun to think of becoming a career math teacher after graduation. I applied for a job in the Fort Wayne, Indiana, public schools, thinking it was an exciting and up-to-date city. From Ft. Wayne, I could make "raids" on the Anderson College campus to go on weekend dates with college girls, but Fort Wayne responded to my application too late, thank God.

Also in spring 1962, I was in a philosophy class taught by Dr. Louis Hennigar. Chubby Checker's song "The Twist" had been popular earlier, and in 1962 Mr. Checker recorded "Let's Twist Again" (... "like we did last summer"). One morning Dr. Hennigar complained to our philosophy class about the popularity of "The Twist" and its sequel. Hennigar thought "The Twist" and entertainment like it were sad commentaries on the low level of American culture. I had never lived outside our American culture, nor had I thought much about the nature of American culture since I was so deeply immersed in it. I didn't fully understand his comment, but it began to raise my curiosity about events and fads in our country and in the big world beyond. I would soon learn more.

My college career as a student politician may have been one of the reasons I was invited in May 1962 to join the Peace Corps. My presence in the Peace Corps would be big news at the college, and it would make the news in my hometown of Elmore, Ohio and in nearby Toledo. My major in math probably helped my chances too.

CHAPTER 2

THE INVITATION

"Bliss it was in that dawn to be alive
But to be young was very heaven."

—William Wordsworth, *The Prelude*

I HAVE SOMETIMES THOUGHT of a person's life as a stream that begins at a small spring in a quiet mountain meadow. At the beginning, our lives seem to move slowly and quietly, and we feel that little is happening. But as you progress into school, the current of the stream quickens and gathers speed as you go through school. You graduate, and the stream leaps over a cliff. You fall on rocks below and rise high in the mist as a beautiful rainbow. Entering the Peace Corps was a defining moment like that for me. Here's how it began.

On a warm, sunny spring day in May 1962, I attended a 9:00 a.m. class and went to the campus mailboxes in the basement of Old Main. What happened next was electrifying and life-changing. Only one piece of mail was in my box that day, and the return address was "Peace Corps, Washington, D.C." I stood in front of my mailbox and tore open the envelope. "Dear

JOURNEY TO ETHIOPIA: 1962-1964

Nyle Kardatzke," the letter began. "Congratulations on. . ." Students swirled around me while I read the whole letter. A response was due in a week.

I was bursting with joy! But the letter said I was being invited to teach in Ethiopia, not Kenya.

"Where is Ethiopia?" I wondered. All I knew about Ethiopia was from an article in *Time* magazine in 1960. A coup to overthrow Emperor Haile Selassie had failed, and I remembered seeing a picture in *Time* of conspirators being hanged after the failed coup. "But where, exactly, is Ethiopia?" I wondered as I scurried across campus to the library.

Kenya, my first choice, was still a colony in 1962, so the Peace Corps was not sending volunteers there. It gained independence in December 1963, and I visited Kenya from Ethiopia the next month.

Encyclopedia Britannica showed that Ethiopia is on the east side of Africa, halfway down the continent. The encyclopedia went on to tell about the history, geography, population, politics, and economy of Ethiopia. It explained more than I could absorb, but it showed me where in the world I would be going.

I learned that Ethiopia was one of the poorest countries in the world, with an average cash income of $30 per person per year. The average life expectancy was twenty-eight years, but much higher for people who lived past age five. One of the oldest monarchies in the world ruled the country and Ethiopia was one of the world's oldest Christian countries in the world. I didn't know what the climate might be, and I had never heard of any of Ethiopia's languages but I wanted to go.

I told a few friends about the Peace Corps invitation and they barely understood what I was saying. I called my parents because they had loaned me money for my last year of college, and I needed to ask for an extension on the loan. My parents must have been jolted by my news, but they took it in stride. They told me not to worry about the money; it could be settled later. They tried to grasp what I was telling them about going to Ethiopia for two years to teach school. My dad said, "It would be a way that you could try to make the world a little better." I detected a trace of skepticism in my dad's voice, but he did describe part of my ambition in that sentence: I wanted to make the world better. Travel and adventure were my other ambitions.

On the weekend before graduation, a swimming pool accident threatened my Peace Corps future. I went to a party at a country club on the west side of Anderson with a local college friend, Paul Anderson, whose parents had a membership at the club. In my giddy excitement, I bounced high off the diving board, dived deep, and hit my head on the bottom of the pool. I came up with blood streaming down my face, and I feared the injury might prevent me from going to Ethiopia, but the bleeding stopped and I recovered quickly.

My graduation on June 18, 1962, was in a newly built concrete dome auditorium on the Anderson College campus. All of the traditional features of a college graduation were there: faculty in robes, caps, and hoods reflecting their highest degrees; graduating students in stifling hot black robes and black mortarboard hats; the parade into the building; a dignitary's speech; and the graduates' brisk walk across the stage for their diplomas and a handshake from the college president. I was blessed and called good that day but only for my college degree, not for a more lofty reason. I was ready to go to Africa for two years. Peace Corp training would start in ten days.

CHAPTER 3

PREPARATIONS

Peace Corps Training

THE PEACE CORPS SENT ME FIRST FROM ANDERSON to Fort Benjamin Harrison in Indianapolis for a physical exam. Driving to the fort was my first Peace Corps journey, and it seemed momentous. A young doctor weighed me, drew some blood, checked my pulse and blood pressure, listened to my breathing, and probably tried to see if I was carrying germs of any contagious diseases. I was a skinny 160-pound twenty-two-year-old, and I passed the physical exam, maybe almost with flying colors.

The Peace Corps sent an FBI agent to interview my neighbors in Anderson. That must have been dull work for the agent. There was nothing exciting or incriminating in my background.

Peace Corps training would start on July 8 at Georgetown University in Washington, D.C. I had been in Washington once before when I was a member of the Future Farmers of America. Back then I was a boy; in 1962, I was a man, or thought I was. One suitcase was enough for the two-month training program.

JOURNEY TO ETHIOPIA: 1962-1964

The flight to Washington, D.C. was the second commercial flight of my life. Two years earlier, I had paid $10 for a one-way flight from Toledo to Cleveland to visit a young woman I was dating. I had wanted the experience of flying, but I could afford only a one-way plane ticket. I took a bus from Cleveland back to Elmore.

For Peace Corps training, the flight to Washington National Airport was on a four-engine, propeller-driven TWA plane. I buckled into a seat for take-off, but during the flight I roamed to a small cocktail lounge with a round table surrounded by a couch. It was elegant seating, but it would not be allowed now.

At the Washington National Airport, I hailed a cab for the first time in my life, but I had seen it done in a few movies. The taxi driver sped through traffic and across the Potomac River, and I was soon standing in front of towering buildings at Georgetown University. Peace Corps representatives were there to greet new volunteers, and I was assigned to a dorm room in Copley Hall. My roommate, Danny Langdon, had already set up camp, but Danny wasn't there, so I went outside to greet other Peace Corps Volunteers as they arrived.

Cabs, private cars, and airport busses arrived and delivered their passengers on the lawn in front of the dorms. One arrival stood out. A long, black limousine arrived, and a tall young man stepped out. I thought he must be rich, judging by his car, and I could tell I was among sophisticated people. I didn't know that even lowly future farmers like me could rent a limousine like that just by shelling out a few more dollars.

Soon after we arrived, pictures were taken of all of us new volunteers, like the pictures our schools had taken of us. Some volunteers said they were like mug shots of criminals when they are first arrested. Most of us looked very young and earnest, and the photos don't lie; we were young and innocent and earnest. Those pictures were compiled into a loose-leaf album we called "The Peace Corps Funny Book." I still have my funny book.

Georgetown was a mind-broadening time. I didn't know any of the other volunteers when I arrived, and I knew only a few when we left for Ethiopia two months later. I met bright people, mostly near my age, and they were from all over the country. A few volunteers may have been as naïve as I was, but most seemed to have more worldly wisdom. Many had graduated from well-known universities, and I was impressed by the big college names. I had to timidly admit that I had graduated from little-known Anderson College in the Midwest. A new friend Talbot (Toby) Page, was a Harvard graduate, and he liked to tease me about coming from "the steppes of Middle America," a place he hadn't visited and didn't hope to see.

Many of the volunteers had graduated from Harvard, Yale, Stanford, UC Berkeley, Northwestern, the University of Wisconsin, and well-known East Coast liberal arts colleges. Coming from Anderson College in the Midwest, I sometimes felt intimidated by the big college names, but we all faced the same challenges in training and in Ethiopia.

The 1962 "Funny Book" shows how young most of us were. Ages twenty-one and twenty-two were the most common, and twenty-five seemed old. A man who was forty-three seemed very old, and one who was fifty seemed really, really old. The old-age winners were Beulah Bartlett, age sixty-five; Blythe Monroe, age sixty-six; and Cora Parrish, age sixty-six. To them, the two years in Ethiopia must have been just an interlude of adventure, not 10 percent of their lives as it was for the younger people.

Our Country Director, Harris Wofford, had overall responsibility for our training and all aspects of our working lives in Ethiopia. He spoke *to us* during training at Georgetown University, and he would speak *for us* later when we met Haile Selassie, Emperor of Ethiopia, in Addis Ababa. Wofford was passionate about civil rights and was a friend of Coretta Scott King, wife of Martin Luther King, Jr. Wofford had worked for Sargent Shriver, the Peace Corps Director, during John Kennedy's presidential campaign in 1960. When Martin Luther King was in jail in Birmingham in September 1960 on a charge of driving with an out-of-state driver's license, he and his family feared for his life. Wofford gave Shriver Mrs. King's phone number, and Shriver passed it on to Kennedy. Kennedy called King in his Birmingham jail cell, and news about Kennedy's call helped protect King. African American votes helped elect Kennedy in November 1960.

Exercise, Food, Lectures, and Medicine

Physical fitness began the first morning at 6:00 a.m. on an athletic field not far from the university dorms. I remember only men out at early morning calisthenics, but maybe I was too innocent to notice young women who may have been there.

JOURNEY TO ETHIOPIA: 1962-1964

Our training leader spoke with a Hungarian accent that added an aura of culture to our sweaty workouts. He blew a whistle at 6:00 a.m., and off we went around the quarter-mile track. For some of us, the morning run became a race. We kept track of our times and our finishing places. After the run, we lined up like military recruits for calisthenics and our Hungarian leader stood in front of us and yelled, "Sideways the arms!" We obediently stretched out our arms and made circles in the air. Next came jumping jacks and other exercises I have long since abandoned to protect my health.

Our military-style morning training later fell out of favor in the Peace Corps and was dropped, but the volunteers who had the "military" training had the highest rate of two-year completions overseas.

After exercises, we had time for showers and a change of clothes before breakfast and morning classes. From the Georgetown dining room, we could look across the Potomac River to a highway leading into Washington from the suburbs. Each morning, cars sped along toward what I thought were dull days in dull offices. The lives of those drivers seemed dull compared to what I was doing in training and what I expected in Ethiopia.

Food in the dining hall at Georgetown tasted good to the Americans, but it was nauseatingly bland for our Ethiopian trainers. Several Ethiopian men were at Georgetown to help train us. More than once, a royal-looking Ethiopian man went to the kitchen and returned to his table with a bottle of Tabasco sauce. He dosed his food with the fiery sauce, and some of the Americans were scandalized. He was ruining the food, they thought. I barely knew what Tabasco was, but it seemed to tell me that the food we would find in-country would be hot.

After our first year in Ethiopia, probably much sooner for some, we understood the Ethiopian disdain for bland American food. An Ethiopian I met in Los Angeles a few years later told me that he forced himself to eat gooey, sticky, bland American cheeseburgers. At first he threw up when he ate a cheeseburger, but he eventually trained himself to eat them. When I first tasted Ethiopian food, it was overwhelmingly spicy. I was used to bland cheeseburgers, so I had to learn to love spicy Ethiopian food, reversing what my Ethiopian friend had done.

Most of the morning lectures faded quickly from my mind, almost before the closing lines were spoken, but I remember the special sessions for the math teachers. We were introduced to "new math" from the School

Mathematics Study Group. The math was "new" by being rooted in axiomatic logic rather than just memorization of algebraic operations. *I used the "new math" in the school at Adi Ugri, and it worked well.*

Paul Tsongas from Massachusetts was a member of the math teachers' group and attended the same lectures. One evening a few of us were chatting outside the men's dormitory when someone asked Paul what he thought of his 30-year-old Massachusetts senator, Ted Kennedy. Young Ted seemed to have ridden into the Senate on his older brother's coattails.

"He's a fool!" Paul said. "He's only there because his brother is sitting in the White House!"

Paul's judgment of Ted Kennedy never came to light publicly, and one can safely assume he didn't discuss it with Senator Kennedy. Paul Tsongas later became the junior senator from Massachusetts, serving with Ted Kennedy in the Senate. Tsongas died in 1997 at the age of fifty-five of non-Hodgkin's lymphoma.

In addition to other subject matter, our Ethiopian trainers introduced us to Amharic, the Ethiopian national language, and its syllabic alphabet. Each sound in Amharic is written as a syllable made up of a consonant root and a short attachment for the vowel sound. We did little writing in our Amharic classes, but we learned basic greetings and the Ethiopian national anthem. *A year later, a few of us living in Eritrea would also learn some Tigrinya, the main language in that part of the country.*

Medical treatment was another aspect of preparing to go to Ethiopia. While at Georgetown, we started taking Aralen chloroquine pills once a week to prevent malaria. The pills were bitter, and we took them at mealtime to avoid the flavor and to avoid upset stomachs. Maybe the bitter taste spread through our bodies and turned away the mosquitoes, especially the ones with malaria. We continued to take Aralen for two years.

To avoid dental emergencies overseas and to provide training for future dentists, crooked or impacted wisdom teeth were removed at the Georgetown Dental School. Two of my wisdom teeth were impacted, meaning they hadn't yet surfaced, so they were surgically removed. I was first dosed with an anesthetic, but I was conscious for the surgery. A young dentist made an incision across the top of a tooth. He placed a chisel on the crown of the tooth, while his assistant stood ready with a small steel hammer.

The dentist said, "Tap, tap," and the assistant hit the chisel just enough to make a groove on the top of the tooth.

When the dentist said, "Split!" the assistant hit the chisel hard and the tooth shattered.

The dentist lifted out pieces of the tooth and then used tongs to pull out the root. He put in a couple of stitches to hold the wound closed, and I was sent back to my room with pain pills.

That afternoon I was reading *Catcher in the Rye,* and my mouth filled with blood each time I laughed. I spat the blood in the toilet each time and kept reading.

Hiking along the Potomac

Besides early morning calisthenics, we were led on a hike along the C&O Canal on a bank of the Potomac River. The hike leader was Supreme Court Justice William O. Douglas, at that time a spry 64-year-old outdoor enthusiast. When the hike stopped for a break, I sat down on the grass next to a young man a little older than most of us. We shook hands, and he said, "Hi. I'm Jay Rockefeller."

"Hi. I'm Nyle Kardatzke," I said. He didn't seem to recognize me or my name.

"Are you related to John D. Rockefeller?" I asked. *I* had heard of *him.*

"Yes, he was my grandfather," Jay Rockefeller affirmed. I took another look at him, and he seemed like a regular guy, even with such a famous name. *He went on to become Governor of West Virginia from 1976 to 1984.*

To toughen us for the rigors of life in Ethiopia, we were taken on a 25-mile hike on the Appalachian Trail in a hilly area east of Washington. On the bus ride to the trailhead, the driver talked with a man who was one of the hike leaders. They talked about hikes they had taken, and the hike leader spoke disparagingly of another hike leader who had forgotten something needed for a hike. I kept quiet. They didn't need to know I had never been on a hike like the one we were starting.

After half a day on the Appalachian Trail, we stopped for the night at a shelter house on the edge of a grassy meadow. Our overseers provided a camping dinner, and they gave each of us a clear plastic sheet for nighttime cover. They gave us no instructions for how we were to bed down for the night with only that plastic sheet. The weather was warm, so we didn't need blankets or sleeping bags, and we were young enough to sleep on the ground without grass pads. We sang folk songs and talked until well after dark. The tall grass in the meadow looked inviting and would provide some padding, so many of us took our plastic sheets and lay down in the soft grass.

The day's hike had tired me enough for good sleep, and I awoke dripping wet when the sun came up. Damp air had settled on the meadow and everything was wet, including the Peace Corps Volunteers. I got up and took my plastic sheet up to a small hill above the meadow where one group had spent the night. It was dry and even a little warmer up on the hill, and the experienced hikers who had spent the night there appeared to be happy and dry. Lesson learned.

That twenty-five mile hike was the longest hike most of us had ever taken, and the longest hike in the lives of some of us, down to the present day.

Meeting President Kennedy at the White House

In summer 1962, six hundred Peace Corps volunteer trainees were in Washington, DC, preparing for assignments around the world. Our Ethiopia group of 310 was the largest the Peace Corps ever sent overseas. A meeting with the president was a highlight of our training time.

When we returned from lunch, several buses were waiting in front of the dorms. We boarded the buses and waited an hour until motorcycle policemen arrived to lead us to the White House. They started their thundering motorcycles and turned on their sirens and led us out onto quiet Georgetown streets. Other police were at every intersection, and we zoomed through all the traffic lights at highway speeds. We were, after all, going to see the President.

White House staff members arranged all the Peace Corps people into a semicircle on the south lawn, facing the White House. We chattered nervously but politely out of respect for where we were.

JOURNEY TO ETHIOPIA: 1962-1964

Four men stepped out onto a balcony above the White House entrance. They wore green cotton suits and were probably heavily armed. I assumed they had machine guns under their suit coats. They looked over the crowd, and one spoke into a walkie-talkie.

Suddenly President Kennedy came from a ground-level door below the armed agents and strode briskly to a podium at the center of our semicircle. Kennedy may have said something inspiring that day, but all I remember is that he invited us to return to Washington and work for the government after our time in the Peace Corps. The invitation wasn't inspiring, to me. I was in the Peace Corps for travel and adventure, not for a government job.

Kennedy then stepped from behind the podium and began to work his way around the semi-circle, shaking hands and talking briefly with volunteers. At close range, I could see that Kennedy was tanned, and his hair was honey-colored, almost red. He was taller than I expected, and he was even better looking than I expected. He was headed toward my roommate, Danny Langdon on the front row. Just before he reached Danny, Kennedy stopped, seemingly finished shaking hands in that direction. He began to turn back, and Danny panicked. He really wanted to speak with Kennedy.

"Mr. President! Mr. President!" Danny yelled.

Those around him were embarrassed at him yelling to the president, but Kennedy stopped and turned back to see who had called to him. He stepped toward Danny, who was shocked that he had shouted to the President.

"Mr. President, ah, Mr. President, ah, what about Ethiopia?" Danny stammered.

"Is that where you are going? To Ethiopia?" Kennedy asked, and extended his hand.

Danny must have said yes, and Kennedy said something I didn't hear and Danny doesn't remember. Danny shook the President's outstretched hand, and the moment of embarrassment was over, covered by Kennedy's gracious pause. Kennedy turned and started back along the line.

As he began to move, Kennedy glanced between the heads of the people in front of me. For an instant, Kennedy made eye contact with me. His eyes were bright blue, and in that instant, I could understand Kennedy's effect on people. I could see why he had been elected president.

"He knows me!" I felt. "He appreciates what I am doing. I'm glad I'm working for him."

Danny Langdon told another volunteer that he didn't wash his hands for a week after shaking hands with Kennedy.

"Rhinoceros" and Race Relations

Our Ethiopia group of PCVs was taken to the Olney Theater in Maryland to see the 1960 avant-garde play "Rhinoceros" by Eugène Ionesco. It was a steamy summer evening, and we were in high spirits. Before the play, some of our group went to a tavern on the theater property for refreshments, but quickly returned to the main group. Some black PCVs had gone to the tavern with group of white PCVs and the black PCVs had been refused service. The entire group walked out and spread the word as they returned to the main group. The tavern became an anathema to our Peace Corps group, and no one went there the rest of the evening.

Ironically, Ionesco's "Rhinoceros" was written as a protest against conformity and mob mentality. In the play, the author protests intellectual isolation and artificiality in academic philosophy. In one scene, a dangerous rhinoceros rampages through the town, and an old philosopher puts his arm across the shoulders of a boy and leads him away, saying, "I'm going to tell you about a syllogism." *A syllogism is a construct in formal logic in which a conclusion is reached from stated facts. It would have been artificial and out of place to discuss philosophy while wild animals were running through the town.*

The little scene at the tavern could have been part of the play had it not been for the PCV's walkout and moral protest.

The CIA

At one point during training, rumors circulated at Georgetown about possible CIA surveillance of volunteers who might be risks to the good name of America. Suspicion focused on a volunteer named Herb who had seemed to lead the protest at the Olney Theater. Rumors circulated that he may have been a CIA plant to affirm that our group would serve the U.S. well in Ethiopia. Peace Corps records report that the man served in the city of Harrar in southeast Ethiopia. If the CIA recommended that any of us be "selected out," I never heard about it.

In 1966, while I was working at Anderson College after my return from Ethiopia, I went to a CIA employment interview in the college library. I thought the CIA might give me a chance for travel and adventure like I had known in the Peace Corps. When I told the interviewer I had been in the Peace Corps, he put down his pen. "I can't talk with you," he said. "We are under strict orders not to hire any former Peace Corps people, and we aren't even to interview them." The Peace Corps wanted to be "squeaky clean" about any relationship to the CIA, so my CIA career ended before it began.

My Uncle Paul Gottke, a World War II bomber pilot, once held a high position at the CIA, and for a time, he was in charge of CIA air operations in Vietnam. He told me of meeting a planeload of Ethiopian soldiers in a jungle landing strip in Asia in the middle of the night during the Korean War. He told me, "A lot of people think government employees don't work very hard. I know the Director of the CIA works hard. Every time I'm in his office on a Saturday morning, he's there."

During training at Georgetown, other rumors circulated among the trainees. Suspicion about who was initiating the rumors turned to a volunteer named John Coyne, who already had a reputation as a creative provocateur. The rumors concerned our date of departure for Ethiopia, our medical care, mismanagement of schedules by the Peace Corps, health threats, and more. At Georgetown and then in Addis Ababa, Coyne was thought to be the source of rumors that were believable, scary, and false. All three of these ingredients made the rumors work. We were all in a state of high anticipation, and the thought of any interruption in our progress toward Ethiopia was unnerving. If the worst of the rumors were true, we might never leave the United States. If we did leave the states, we might be sickened by a dangerous disease. We did in fact face some hazards and uncertainty, but reality was better than those unfounded rumors.

John Coyne became a prolific writer, and he continues his writing to this day. At a Peace Corps conference in about 2000, he advised PCVs, "If you want to write your own book, write 1,000 words every day."

Seeing the Shrink

While at Georgetown, we all were interviewed by psychiatrists. My psychiatrist was a nervous little lady in her sixties. Her hands trembled, and she smoked cigarettes non-stop as she spoke. She noticed that I had respectable grades in college and had even been a student politician, but I had a grade of "F" in freshman orientation. This fact stood out to her and seemed to be a symptom of a psychiatric disorder, so she asked me about that "F" grade. I explained that I had been working full time at night and had gone to bed after 2:00 a.m. every night. I had slept through the 9:00 a.m. Freshman Orientation lectures enough times to be awarded the "F" grade. The psychiatrist accepted my explanation and didn't have me kicked out of the Peace Corps. For that, I was grateful.

Other Excursions

We were taken on several excursions while we were at Georgetown, some more interesting to me than others. At a large public swimming pool one evening, I noticed there were shapely girls in the Peace Corps. We also went to an amusement park and rode a roller coaster. The car would race toward an overhead beam and dive down at the last moment. I escaped death by roller coaster, but other brushes with death lay ahead.

One hot afternoon, I joined a group of Peace Corps people for a walk into the Georgetown shops just outside the university. I followed them into a tavern that lay below street level under a restaurant. Air conditioning was still a rarity. I sat across a table from Herb Segal, a jovial man from California. We chatted a little, and he discovered I had never had a beer in my life.

"Well!" he said, "we need to fix that!"

He called to a waitress, "Bring this guy a beer!"

I was soon staring at a mug of beer that seemed to hold a quart of the amber fluid.

"Take a drink of that!" Herb instructed. "I want to see you have your first beer."

I picked up the mug and tipped it enough to get a sip of the cool liquid. It was a strange, new flavor. It wasn't sweet, and it wasn't tart like lemonade, and it wasn't as nasty as I thought beer might be. My head was spinning just knowing I was having a new experience. I managed to drink more of the beer, and I had no trouble walking back to my dorm, so I decided I must not be drunk. It was my first taste of beer, and it wasn't my last.

Getting Ready to Leave

I had set foot outside the United States only twice before I went to Ethiopia. When I was a boy, my family had gone to Niagara Falls and had crossed to the Canadian side. Everyone visiting the falls looked like Americans, so if I saw any Canadians, I didn't know it. On another family trip, we entered Mexico at Tijuana. The sights there were exotic and almost overwhelming, but I suffered no culture shock the afternoon we were there. The rest of the world outside America was unknown but appealing. I was eager to get out of the country again.

Near the end of training at Georgetown, passport photos were taken, and most of us saw the first passport photos of our young lives. My photo showed me bedraggled and tired, much more realistic than I would have liked, but it vouched for me and made me a legal foreign traveler.

When training ended at Georgetown, we had a week to go home, pack for two years, say goodbye to family and friends, and regroup in New York for our flight to Ethiopia. On the final day at Georgetown, we were to receive tickets for our flights home and from home to New York City. A temporary ticket office had been set up at Georgetown University, but by late morning, only a few tickets had been delivered. (Tickets were all on paper and had to be delivered to the site.) Panic spread among the volunteers, and we didn't show our best manners when we pressed the poor lady in the ticket office about our tickets. When our tickets did arrive, she was happy to hand the tickets over and have us off her hands.

My flight home, from Washington to Toledo, was a near-death Peace Corps experience. About thirty minutes into the flight, a mysterious fog invaded the passenger cabin, creeping along the floor and then rising to passengers' knees. I knew I could die while in the Peace Corps, but I hoped I wouldn't die this way. I hadn't even made it out of the country yet. The flight attendants had no explanation, and the plane made an unscheduled stop at Pittsburgh. A quick check revealed that the fog had something to do with the air conditioning, was harmless, and would soon dissipate. We were soon on our way, and that was another time I didn't die in the Peace Corps.

In Ohio, I had time with family. After church one night, I walked my Grandma Kardatzke to her house next door. She was 79 years old, and her health was failing.

"I don't think I'll live much longer," she sighed, "but I'm ready to go." I said something encouraging that she ignored. She died six months later.

A frenzy of shopping and packing filled the final few days before the overseas flight. Volunteers were allowed two pieces of luggage plus a small flight bag. A footlocker of added clothing would be shipped separately, and the Peace Corps would supply a footlocker of paperback books. Near the end of the week at home, the visiting and packing time seemed short. Too soon, it seemed, it was time to go to the airport.

My dad and older brother were at work at the Sun Oil refinery in Toledo, so my mother was in charge of my departure. She gathered my younger four siblings and me in our living room, and we all knelt at chairs to pray. My mother started the prayer time, and my siblings each prayed, starting with my eight-year-old sister, Annette. When it was my turn to pray, I started my prayer asking for safety for me and the family in the two years that lay ahead. Suddenly the reality of the two years struck me, and I realized that some of us might die before my return. I burst into tears, sobbing at the thought. My mother and my brothers and sisters cried too.

My little sister Annette, seeing all of us crying, asked, "Why is everybody crying? He's not going to *die*, is he?"

We all laughed through our tears, and our prayer time was over.

The plane from Toledo to New York was a DC-4, a bulky, four-engine, propeller-driven plane. The engines roared and shook the plane, and it lumbered slowly down the runway to its takeoff speed. I could see my family at the airport fence, and they were there waving to me. The plane climbed slowly toward its cruising altitude, but when we flew over the village of Lindsey, Ohio it was still low enough for me to see the old farmhouse where I had been born in 1939. The house was gone when I returned in 1964.

CHAPTER 4

DEPARTURES AND ARRIVALS

From New York to Addis Ababa

THE FLIGHT TO NEW YORK was uneventful, and the Peace Corps had arranged hotel rooms for all who were to fly out the next morning. After dinner, we settled down for a nervous, restless night, and early the next morning, we were out on the street to board buses for Idlewild International Airport. The TWA terminal at Idlewild International Airport was a red-carpeted, futuristic building with swooping ceilings and staircases. Our flight would be on a 707 jet, one of TWA's first jets. We would fly from Idlewild to Rome and then to Athens for the flight to Ethiopia.

Taking off from Idlewild, I had a window seat and watched the marsh grasses at the edge of the runway slip under our heavily loaded plane. Faster and faster we rolled, but we were still on the ground. *How long can this runway be?* I wondered. Suddenly the plane rose, and in an instant marsh grass and water flashed under the plane. When we had been airborne for an hour, I went to the cockpit to visit with the pilots. (Ours was a charter flight, so security on the plane was light. Those were the days before hijackings.)

"It looked as though we didn't have much room to spare when we took off," I said to the pilot.

The pilot nodded, "It was close."

I was so excited that I stood up nearly halfway across the Atlantic, looking out the windows alternately on both sides of the plane. The cockpit door was open, so I went in and talked with the pilots and the navigator. I could see nothing but blue sky from the windshield, but the navigator tracking our course knew where we were. He looked at the sky through a window in the plane's ceiling, using celestial navigation to keep the plane on course.

Entering the Rome airport was my first moment in Europe, and it was a thrill. During a brief fueling stop in Rome, we were dazzled by the gift shops inside the terminal. We had only enough time to use the restrooms and stretch our legs before we were back on the plane.

We landed in Athens in the early morning hours, long before sunrise. We checked into our hotel and were told we could sleep there all day if we wanted. We were to be in Athens only a day while Ethiopian Airlines could assemble enough planes to fly all of us to Addis Ababa. I was so excited to be in Athens that I walked to the Acropolis at the first dim light of day. I knew of the Acropolis because as a young kid I had seen photos and paintings of it in *National Geographic Magazine*. I couldn't wait to see the real thing.

I hiked with a few other Peace Corps people to the Parthenon just as the sun was rising. The ancient temple gleamed in the morning sun, just as I had imagined it would. We hiked up to the Acropolis and looked down on the Agora, an open space where philosophical debates took place in classical times. Looking another direction, the city of Athens was awakening and inviting us to visit. We hiked down and began to explore the city.

At lunch time, a few of us wandered into an ancient, cave-like restaurant. The food was good, but the only thing I remember was a very sweet white wine we sipped as we waited for food. I must have learned something from that glass of wine. Until that day, the only wine I had tasted was dark blue Mogen David wine.

At the Athens airport that evening, several Ethiopian Airlines planes were waiting for us on the tarmac. They were all propeller-driven, four-engine planes with rotary piston engines like the planes I had ridden in the States. Some of the planes flew nonstop from Athens to Addis Ababa, but one or two smaller planes went first to Khartoum in the Sudan before reaching Addis. Unlike the jet that had brought us to Athens, our propeller plane from Athens flew at a relatively low altitude and was repeatedly lifted and dropped by air currents. We felt our plane rising and falling gently as we flew south. Some of the PCVs must have had air sickness, but most of us just felt the plane rising and falling. The flight took nearly 17 hours and we kept feeling the ground rising and falling beneath us during our first days in Addis Ababa.

Our arrival in Ethiopia would be historic, since our plane would be the first Peace Corps plane to land. Some kind of ceremony might be held, so we PCVs thought we should be prepared. Someone suggested that we sing the Ethiopian national anthem. We had sung the national anthem at Georgetown, but no one remembered more than a few phrases. By the odd biology of the brain, the entire national anthem had lodged in my mind. I quickly wrote out a few copies of the words transcribing the Amharic language of the anthem into a phonetic version for our use. The words were passed along through the plane, and we practiced singing the national anthem on the plane.

When the plane dipped below the clouds, we had our first views of Ethiopia. Mountains, valleys, and villages slipped beneath us, and we could see the city in a valley between mountains. The landing was gentle, and we stepped down the stairs in clear, cold, mountain air. A photographer lined us up beside the plane, and we did our best to sing the national anthem in Amharic.

JOURNEY TO ETHIOPIA: 1962-1964

Photo of the group on the ground

Here is the transliteration of the Amharic we used, along with the English translation:

Ityopya hoy des ybelish	Ethiopia, be happy
beamlakish ḣayl benguśish	thanks to the power of God and your ruler.
tibaberawal arbanyochish	Your brave citizens are unanimous;
ayna kam keto netsanetesh	your freedom will never be touched,
bertu nachewna terarochish	as your mountains are defiant
ateferim keṭelatochish	and your natives do not fear any enemy.
del adragiw ngusachin	Long live our victorious ruler
ynurelen lekebrachin	to the glory of our country.
bertu nachewna terarochish	Your mountains are defiant
ateferim keṭelatochish	and your natives do not fear any enemy.
del adragiw ngusachin	Long live our victorious ruler
ynurelen lekebrachin	to the glory of our country

First Views of Addis Ababa

On the bus ride into Addis Ababa from the airport, I had my first moment of culture shock. The road was crowded with people walking, many of them carrying bags of belongings on their backs or balancing them on their heads. Some were guiding loaded donkeys by their halters or pushing loaded wheelbarrows. Some had belongings tied up in bandanas that dangled from walking sticks slung over one shoulder. Some who were not carrying things laid their walking sticks across their shoulders and draped their arms over the sticks.

We had met Ethiopians during training, and I had African American college friends but here *everyone* on the road was dark-skinned. Not only were they dark-skinned, but they weren't wearing Western style slacks, jackets, and dresses. White cloth shawls were draped across their shoulders, folded in a striking, dramatic way. And people were all walking, walking, walking, in a multitude. Bicycles and motorcycles and a few cars crept slowly through the crowd. We had already seen a lot when we arrived at the university.

For our three-week stay at the University College, we were assigned our own individual dormitory rooms, each with a single bed, chair, small desk, and place to put our luggage. I'm not a naturally tidy person, but I was especially tidy in that dorm room. I felt I needed a well-ordered place as a refuge from the unfamiliar jumble of sights, sounds, and smells in the city outside. I needed to establish a "base camp" in my room, and tidiness helped me adapt to the unfamiliar sights and sounds of the city.

Showering in the dorm was an adjustment. Mornings were cold in high-altitude Addis Ababa, and the scene in the men's shower room each morning looked like a scene from a Soviet prison in Siberia. There was hot water, and a cloud of steam swirled around the naked young men getting quickly in and out of the showers.

The first breakfast was another scene from a prison movie. Cooks in white uniforms toiled in the kitchen, and we took metal trays and filed past a serving counter for food. The cooks tried to please us with a breakfast of scrambled eggs and American-style bread. We recognized the scrambled eggs, but they were severely overcooked. Still, eggs with bread and tea were nutritious and got us through that first day.

The scrambled eggs were a major concession to our American habits. In two years, I never saw local Eritreans eat eggs in any form except hard-boiled.

We had arrived in September 1962, in the rainy season, and low-hanging clouds made Addis Ababa look especially dramatic and mysterious. The scent of wood fires and eucalyptus trees added to the aura of adventure. Rain sometimes came at night but surrendered to clear mornings. Afternoon rain usually came at about 2:30 p.m. and lasted an hour or two. On a few days, the rain was nearly continuous, day and night. One rainy night, we were guests for dinners in homes of local Ethiopians. As the rain roared down on my host's corrugated roof, he explained that thieves sometimes broke into houses during heavy rains because people yelling for help usually couldn't be heard.

Within a week of our arrival in Addis Ababa, there was a dinner reception for us in a large hotel. High-level government officials mingled with us, and waiters made sure drinks flowed freely. A server placed a large drinking glass in front of me and filled it half full with what I later learned was Scotch Whisky. Unfamiliar as I was with such ways of the world, I drank the whisky too fast. I didn't faint, and I had a pleasant, dreamy sensation. We were escorted to waiting buses and made it safely back to our dorms at the University College.

Addis Ababa was a sprawling international city. One of the PCVs discovered a Chinese restaurant near the city's center and took us there. The Chinese food was excellent, but we wondered if the restaurant was an outpost of the Chinese government. Someone in our group jokingly suggested the place might be bugged with hidden microphones, but we laughed, uneasily. We never found out whether the restaurant was bugged. After all, it would have been a secret.

In Addis Ababa we began to hear Amharic spoken in shops and in the streets. We knew only a few words and a few sentences in Amharic, but we were glad to recognize at least a few of the sounds around us. A volunteer named Rick Knox was able to put together two sentences that a few of us recited together when we walked to the American embassy one rainless afternoon. We would say to each other, "*Americawi Embassy yet now?*" ("Where is the American embassy?"), and "*Feet la feet heed ina weda keyne zur.*" ("Go straight ahead and turn right.") We were amused by our own feeble attempts to speak Amharic, but it was a start.

Another Amharic word we learned, was *ishi*. The word means "okay" in Amharic, and it's as common in Ethiopian conversation as "okay" is in

American English. *Ishi nega* means "okay, tomorrow." We were told it was like saying *mañana*, in Spanish-speaking countries.

Free Time and Planned Excursions

The Peace Corps staff and local Ethiopian trainers had planned a busy schedule of sight-seeing and lectures, but we also had free time to explore the city. We could walk from the University College to shops in the center of Addis Ababa, but we sometimes caught rides in tiny taxis that darted by. The standard taxi fare was "one simuni." A *simuni* was a copper coin the size of an American quarter that was worth 25 cents in Ethiopian money, the equivalent of ten cents in American money. If we shared the cab with other riders, everyone paid a *simuni*, but there was no tipping.

On walks into the center of Addis, multilingual street peddlers met us. Each peddler had a shallow box suspended in front of his stomach by a strap around his neck. There were cigarettes in the bag but also chewing gum, Band-Aids, individual packets of aspirin, needles with thread, ballpoint pens, tiny notebooks, combs, bars of soap, and much more. Prices were so low that it didn't seem humane to try to bid them down, but you could bargain in at least four languages. All the peddlers spoke Amharic, but nearly all could also do business in Italian. Some spoke a little French, perhaps due to the French presence in Djibouti on the east coast. Many peddlers also spoke Arabic because of the many Muslims and visitors from Arabia. And most peddlers seemed able to do business in Oromo, Tigrinya, Tigre, and other Ethiopian languages. Most of the street vendors also knew a smattering of English, the world's most widely spoken language, and the English-speaking customers usually seemed to have spending money. This wonderful mix of languages was an open invitation for us to join in, buy and sell, greet, and thank people while making a spectacle of ourselves in the languages of our choice.

During our stay in Addis Ababa, we were taken on bus excursions outside the city to see the Ethiopian countryside. One trip took us to a sugar processing plant where stalks of sugar cane were crushed by huge steel wheels. The juice was cooked to evaporate water and make sugar crystals.

We were also taken to one of Haile Selassie's country homes for tea and cookies, and we saw the small chapel where the emperor sometimes knelt to pray. Heavy clouds hung over brooding mountains, and Ernie Fox, an especially articulate member of our Peace Corps group, exclaimed "This country just *stinks* with beautiful scenery!"

He meant it as a compliment.

The word expatriate was not in my vocabulary before I went to Ethiopia, but that's what I and my fellow PCVs were. Expatriates are simply people living outside their native countries. While living in Ethiopia, we were immersed in sights, sounds, smells, and flavors we couldn't have experienced back in Ohio, Minnesota, California, or other home states. Making us expatriates was one of the greatest gifts the Peace Corps gave us.

Meeting the "King of Kings"

We were the first Peace Corps Volunteers in Ethiopia, so we were celebrities of sorts. The Peace Corps was new, and Ethiopia had friendly relations with the United States. Soon after our arrival in Addis Ababa, we were invited to the Imperial Palace to be greeted by His Imperial Majesty, Haile Selassie. There may have been a few snorts from PCVs who felt it would violate their democratic convictions if they met with an emperor. I had no such scruples. I wanted to meet Haile Selassie.

At our dorms, we were within walking distance of the palace, but transportation was arranged for us in big, blue Mercedes buses. We were free to roam outside the palace and explore the grounds before we were taken inside. Behind the palace was a zoo-style steel cage and a mature female lion was inside. The cage door opened easily, and a few of us went inside the cage with the lion. Fortunately, the lion was peaceful and did not eat any of us. The Lord must have kept the lion's mouth closed, as He did in the Bible story about Daniel, the prophet in a den of lions.

The Peace Corps group was directed inside the palace to a large reception hall. At one end of the room, Emperor Haile Selassie stood on a small, raised dais in front of an ornate throne. He was wearing a white military uniform, and there was a wide ribbon across his chest. With the dignity of an emperor, he looked above our heads toward the back of the room, not directly at us. A tall, bald, Ethiopian man in a European style suit was standing beside the Emperor. The man seemed to be an advisor to the emperor, possibly a military man or a diplomat. On the emperor's other side were more officials. The emperor's nervous little Chihuahua dog stood at his feet and looked at the crowd suspiciously as if to protect his royal owner.

When the PCVs were assembled and quiet, Emperor Haile Selassie raised a document and began to read his greeting. We were told he was fluent in French and English, but he read his greeting to us in Amharic. Someone repeated the greeting in English for us, but merely hearing the emperor speak was impressive.

While Haile Selassie was reading, his little Chihuahua started barking at the audience. The tall military man hissed at the dog.

"Pssst!" he said in the Ethiopia way of saying, "Shhh!"

The dog kept barking.

Haile Selassie stopped reading his speech and looked down at his dog.

"Pssst!" the emperor hissed, and the Chihuahua dropped silently to the floor for the rest of the speech.

After the Emporer's greeting, we were invited to file in front of the emperor and shake his hand. His hand was tiny and delicate, and he held his imperial composure when each of us took his hand. He was, after all, an emperor. The little dog looked at each of us and held his peace.

When Haile Selassie finished his speech, an official stepped forward and announced that refreshments would be served. Tall glasses of champagne appeared along with tiny sandwiches and other hors d'oeuvres. We nibbled respectfully and sipped champagne, some of us for the first time, as we tried to take in what we were seeing in the royal meeting hall.

Before dark, we were back at the University College for dinner, still dressed in suits and ties and still marveling at our historic meeting.

Calling Haile Selassie the emperor was not just for show: it had real political meaning. Ethiopia was in fact an empire, since it was made up of several individual nations, each with its own history and its own royal authorities. One of Haile Selassie's titles, "King of Kings," referred to the fact that he ruled over those many kingdoms through the power of the local kings. The devout Haile Selassie would not have seen his title, "King of Kings," as an insult to Christ, who also was called "King of Kings." For Haile Selassie, King of Kings was a purely secular title.

I took lots of pictures during our audience with Haile Selassie, but I lost all of them when I trusted an American soldier to mail my film to my parents through military mail. God alone knows what he did with my film. The photo below was taken by one of the other Ethiopia volunteers.

Letters Home

Letter writing was my main link to home while I was living so far away for two years. My family had a history of letter writing because it was the best way my mother could communicate from our home in Ohio with her mother in Oklahoma. Postage was cheap, and phone calls were too expensive for anything but emergencies like a death in the family.

The most valuable practical skill I learned in high school was typing—real typing, not one-finger, hunt-and-peck typing. Mrs. Barker, the typing teacher in Elmore, led our class through drills for touch typing, and we picked up speed as the year went along. By the end of the year I could type at the blazing speed of 42 words per minute, fast enough for writing my college term papers. My typed papers made me look more intelligent than my illiterate handwriting would have suggested.

I would need a typewriter for my letters from Ethiopia, and I found a small Olivetti typewriter at a shop in Asmara. It was the smallest typewriter I have ever used, but the full-size keyboard was like all the others. I could clatter away typing lessons for my students and writing letters to my parents and other family members and friends. I left the Olivetti in Eritrea.

I wrote lots of letters at my home in Adi Ugri, often writing during the 2½-hour lunch break. The letters I sent home were on special stamped stationery sold by the Adi Ugri post office. Called Aerograms, they were extremely low weight. I could type nearly two pages of information on an Aerogram by typing on the main section and on two flaps that were folded in before mailing. The Aerograms were light blue in color and they had a colorful margin. An Ethiopian stamp was part of the Aerogram itself. By typing fast I could fill an Aerogram and take it to the post office in time for the afternoon mail pickup.

My parents saved my Aerograms, and I still have some of those letters. It seems that Aerograms no longer exist. They may have become obsolete when the weight of letters became trivial on massive jet airplanes.

When I went to the Adi Ugri post office, a young man named Asfeha handed over my mail, sold me stamps, and chatted with me cautiously. The postmaster was an older man who didn't speak a word of English, at least not to me. One day I saw the old man wash up before lunch, splashing water over his head and hands and letting water splatter on the floor. Asfeha smiled at me lamely. When the old man left, I said, "Who's going to clean that up?"

"I am," Asfeha replied. We both smiled and let the matter drop.

I wrote lots of letters in my two years overseas, but I never made a phone call to my family in the States in those two years.

While I was teaching in Adi Ugri, I wanted my students to have the experience of letter writing, and a few of them wrote to pen pals I found for them in the States. I helped them edit their letters, recommending changes in letters that mentioned the "Piss Crops" and the "Peace Corpse."

CHAPTER 5

TO ERITREA IN THE NORTH

WHEN WE HAD BEEN IN ADDIS ABABA for a couple of weeks, the Peace Corps leaders told us where we had been assigned for our first year of teaching. I was one of sixty PCVs assigned to Eritrea. What I knew about Eritrea wouldn't have filled a teacup, but I was ready for another leap into the unknown. I only knew that Eritrea was a province of Ethiopia and that it had been an Italian colony. I knew next to nothing of how Eritrea was affected by its presence on the Red Sea and so near to Arabia. When I left Eritrea in 1964, I knew enough to fill a good-sized teacup of knowledge, and I also loved Eritrea and Eritreans.

Eritrea is a semi-desert, and an occasional dust storm blows in as a reminder that the Sahara Desert is just to the west. Eritrea receives enough rain for Teff and a few other grains, and irrigated farms produce oranges, bananas, and other tropical fruit. South of Eritrea is the great, historic country of Ethiopia, vastly larger than Eritrea, but related to Eritrea by history, language, religion, culture, diet, and geography.

Eritrea had become an Italian colony in 1889 and had served as a base for Benito Mussolini's invasion of Ethiopia in 1935. A British army from Sudan invaded Eritrea in 1941 early in World War 2, expelled the Italian government, and made Eritrea a British protectorate. As a result of its years as an Italian colony, the culture and architecture of Eritrea was Italian, and many Italian families had lived there for three or four generations. Its future was unclear in 1962 when our Peace Corps group arrived.

We flew to Eritrea in early September on an Ethiopian Airlines flight from Addis Ababa to Asmara. I was seated next to a Greek merchant who was on his way to Athens. He didn't speak English, so I tried my beginner's French on him. He replied in simplified French, and there I was, actually using my two years of college French. I didn't use French again until two years later when I spoke to a man at the Coliseum in Rome on my way home.

At the Asmara airport, an Eritrean photographer took pictures of us as we crossed the tarmac into the terminal. In his photo of me, I was beaming, leaning forward earnestly, with a camera and flight bag dangling from my neck. I was a poster child of a well-washed, naïve American plunging into a new culture.

The camera dangling from my neck was a Zeiss Ikon 35-mm that I had bought just before I left Ohio. It could focus manually for close-ups and could make time exposures. I later bought a Canonflex RM single lens reflex camera from an American military friend. The Canon made a loud noise when its lens opened and a black screen inside was raised for a fraction of a second to expose the film. I used the Canon for color slides and relegated the Zeiss to black and white photos for prints. *The Zeiss Ikon was later stolen from my office at UCLA when I was a graduate teaching assistant there.*

Asmara was another new cultural experience. It was a mixture of the 1890s and 1962. I was charmed by the European feel of the city. A Catholic church was the largest building on Haile Selassie I Avenue, and it made Asmara seem like part of Italy.

My first *pensione,* an Italian boarding house, was on Haile Selassie I Avenue. The chimes from the church just two blocks up the street added to the aura of Italy. The church had been built before the First World War, and the palm-lined streets must have been laid out then, too. Asmara was small enough for walking, but there were horse-drawn buggies called *gharries* that offered taxi rides for a low price. The clip-clop of the *gharry* ponies was like music in the streets. There were cars, of course, but I had seen cars before.

Haile Selassie I Avenue and the Catholic church

In our first days in Asmara, we went for lunch in the home of Eritrean hosts. PCV Linda Hughes and I had an Eritrean lunch in the home of a government official. He took us around the city and also showed us a many sights, including a place where Hindus from India cremated the bodies of their family members.

In Asmara, I shared a room in a pensione with Steve Chesebrough, a man I hadn't met at Georgetown. I didn't realize until later that Steve was a Harvard man. I had heard, "You can always tell a Harvard man, but you can't tell him much," but neither part of that saying was true in Steve's case. He was as amiable as any college man could be.

I began to learn about bargaining over prices in my earliest days in Asmara. At a shop on a side street, I paid $2.00 *Ethi* for a crude local broom made from a tree branch with a bundle of stiff leaves tied at one end. I soon learned that the local price for that kind of broom was 25 cents *Ethi*, or 10 cents American. I had paid eight times the going price for that broom. Prices in the larger stores in Asmara seemed fixed and not open to negotiation. At the Greek grocery store, we never haggled over the prices.

JOURNEY TO ETHIOPIA: 1962-1964

Asmara, capital of Eritrea, was a little piece of Italy in the early 1960s. Italian restaurants there ranged from elegant and slightly pricey to lower cost but very good. Menghetti's was the most elegant, but the Capri was our favorite. There was also an Eritrean restaurant on a side street where I learned to love Eritrean injera and zigini.

After a week in Asmara, we were taken to our new homes. Those assigned to schools in Asmara were moved to houses or apartments the Peace Corps had arranged. Those of us going to villages were taken with our luggage in a small Peace Corps pickup truck to our new homes.

Coffee shops were a new cultural experience for me as a former FFA boy from Ohio. I had grown up drinking drip-grind Folger's coffee with milk and sugar and had never heard of café latte or espresso coffee, but the dark-roasted Italian coffees were easy to love. All the coffee shops served Italian pastries, and no trip to Asmara was complete without at least one stop at a coffee shop.

The Greek grocery store supplied foreigners with canned goods for American or European cooking. There were canned goods and fresh vegetables, and barrels of ripe olives proved the place was really Greek. On another side street a clean, modern butcher shop would sell us any cut of meat we wanted . . . for a price. Other stores sold clothing, hardware, pots and pans, and most other things we thought we needed.

Asmara was the home of Melotti Beer, which many Americans thought must be a joke: Italian beer? But Melotti was the beer of choice for most foreigners, and it was much cheaper than imported European beer.

The Peace Corps rented "the Peace Corps transient house" in Asmara for weekend use by Peace Corps people who came in from outlying villages. I was at the transient house for my first earthquake. Four of us had just begun to eat when the stone house vibrated and began a low-pitched, humming sound. Bill Kerske, from Southern California, yelled, "Earthquake! Get out!"

We followed Bill out into the street and saw people running from other houses. No one wanted to be buried under a pile of rubble if their house caved in. I had grown up in a part of Ohio where there had not been an earthquake in living memory, so this was my first earthquake and it was not the last one in Eritrea.

In 1962, parts of Ethiopia had not been accurately mapped, but in 1963 detailed mapping was begun by the Ethiopian and US governments. At the Asmara airport in spring 1964, I had a close look at a huge prop-driven US military transport plane. Inside was a giant camera with a giant lens that took pictures of the

Eritrean-Ethiopian countryside as the plane flew over. The Ethiopia-US Mapping Mission was activated in July 1963, and during its lifespan involved about a thousand U.S. military and civilian personnel. Mapping was completed in July 1970.

Eritrean and Ethiopian Names

Eritrean and Ethiopian personal names, follow a generational pattern, unlike the Western system of names where the father's last name is taken by his wife at marriage and is passed down to his children and later descendants. The father's last name becomes the last name of his children. Ethiopians and Eritreans do not have surnames, or "last names." Instead, an Ethiopian man's personal name is followed by his father's personal name. The names are not like "Smith," "Jones," or my favorite, "Kardatzke." If I were an Ethiopian, my name would be "Nyle Arlin" because Arlin Kardatzke is my father's first and last name. His father's first and last name was Fred Kardatzke, so in Ethiopia I might also be known as "Nyle Arlin Fred." The process continues for generations.

Ethiopian and Eritrean names have meanings. They aren't just labels like most of our American names. My friend Yemane Russom has a lovely name. "Yemane" means "at my right hand." "Russom" means "the king." So "Yemane Russom" means "at the right hand of the king." A girl in my homeroom class was named "Tsehainesh," which means "my sunshine." Her father's name was Ghebrejohannes, which means "the servant of John," so she was "my sunshine, the servant of John."

The most famous Ethiopian name is "Haile Selassie." He was born a prince and at his birth he was named "Lij (prince) Tafari Makonen." When he became Emperor, he took the title "Haile Selassie," which means "the power of the Trinity." As if that title weren't enough, he had other titles: Emperor of Ethiopia, Elect of God, King of Kings, and Two Hundred Twenty-fifth King in the Solomonic Line. You're not likely to see a democratically elected Head of State with a title like that.

Weekends in Asmara

When school started, our weeks were punctuated by frequent, weekend bus trips up to Asmara. Asmara is at a higher altitude, and it is north of Adi

Ugri, so it was "up" in two ways. [The paved road to Asmara wound up and through forty miles (54 kilometers) of spectacular mountain scenery.] The attractions in Asmara included restaurants, movie theaters, coffee shops, a barber shop, grocery stores, and the large Catholic church. The American military base at Kagnew Station offered a few comforts of home for those who had a friend on the base. The Odeon Theater downtown usually showed American movies in English, but sometimes the movies were from India or Italy. Subtitles ran above and below the screen in Amharic, Tigrinya, Arabic, Italian, and English.

In Asmara restaurants, we ordered bottled drinking water with our meals. It could be carbonated ("with gas," it was called) or not carbonated, but most foreigners chose carbonated drinking water. Non-carbonated water could have been un-boiled tap water in a bottle that had once contained commercially purified water. Untreated tap water could give you diarrhea or amoebic dysentery.

Curio shops in Asmara sold keepsakes that were fancier than those in most local marketplaces. The olive wood bowls for sale had been turned on a lathe because the wood was so hard it couldn't be carved any other way. We were told that the only other wood as hard as Eritrean olive wood was found in Israel. I never heard it suggested that Israeli olive wood may have descended from plants taken there by the Queen of Sheba, but that seems plausible.

On one weekend bus trip, the Adi Ugri -bound bus with passengers aboard had to go to a large garage in Asmara for a repair. About one hundred people were seated in the garage, in a meeting, and they took turns raising questions and making comments. A man on the bus told me that they were shareholders in the corporation that owned the bus company. Capitalism was alive and well in Eritrea.

Some of the buses that ran between Asmara and Adi Ugri may have been built in the 1930s before the Italians invaded Ethiopia. Those ancient buses were blue and looked like inflated balloons. They had their place on the roads along with shiny new Mercedes buses.

There was a rivalry between two bus companies on the road between Asmara and Adi Ugri. I once saw two buses, one from each company, race to pick up passengers. At each stop, the conductor on our bus would jump out and run ahead of the other bus to "kidnap" passengers who were in line to board the first bus. I didn't see any passengers injured, and the passengers on both buses enjoyed the show.

I once saw several crates of strawberries waiting to be loaded onto a bus at the Adi Ugri bus station, but never saw strawberries for sale in the Adi Ugri market. They must have been raised in farms nearby, possibly still run by Italians. Strawberries were not part of the usual Eritrean diet, so they may have been for foreigners or Eritrean urbanites in Asmara, or possibly for export to Europe.

CHAPTER 6

ADI UGRI

Adi Ugri, aka Mendefera, Our New Hometown

OUR SMALL TRIBE of five Peace Corps teachers could not have been assigned to a more beautiful, interesting city than Adi Ugri. The weather was wonderful most of the time because the town was about a mile above sea level, and it was so close to the equator that it received nearly direct sunlight. Daytime temperatures were in the 80s Fahrenheit in the dry season, and nights were in the 50s. At 54 kilometers (40 miles) south of Asmara, the town was an easy hour and a half bus trip from urban shopping and restaurants in the city.

Mendefera, the alternate name for Adi Ugri, means "who dares it?" According to a legend, the valley where the town sits was once infested with lions. No one would spend a night in the valley, and no one dared to build a house there. One man, not knowing the danger, built a small house and started a fire to ward off the mountain chill. A person walking around the edge of the dangerous valley saw the smoke and declared, *"Mendefera?" (Who dares it?)*

That's how the place became Mendefera, but the Italians gave it another name later: Adi Ugri. "Adi" means "village" in Tigrinya. "Ugri" means "deep dialog" or "meaningful dialog." There may have been deep negotiations for the land when the town was expanded in Italian times.

The Peace Corps rented two houses for our group of five teachers. The houses were empty when we first saw them, but simple furniture arrived that day. All five of us, two men and three women, went to work sanding and varnishing the new furniture. The smell of fresh varnish made our houses seem more up to date than most of the others in our new hometown.

In both houses, each teacher had a a desk, a single bed, a chest of drawers for socks and underwear, and a free-standing wardrobe for hanging clothes. There was also a couch and two sitting room chairs in each house. The chairs had pads filled with some sort of dense fiber.

Each kitchen had a table and four chairs, a kerosene stove, and a kerosene refrigerator. *I was amazed that a little flame at the bottom of the refrigerator could produce ice at the top and keep food cold in between. I was a good enough mechanic to keep the refrigerators going in both houses, mainly by keeping the refrigerators level and their wicks clean. We made ice from boiled water, but I still don't understand how a flame can make ice.*

Bill Kerske and I lived in the two-bedroom stone-walled house in town that we all called "the boys' house." Between the two bedrooms was the kitchen that served as our dining room. A hallway along the front of the house connected the kitchen to the two large bedrooms. The three Peace Corps women lived in a two-story house on the school compound that we called "the girls' house," and they had the same kind of furniture as the boys.

In the first year, 1962 to 1963, Bill Kerske and I both had our beds in one large room and used the other large room for a sitting, reading, and entertaining room. Bill moved to Asmara for the second year, and John Rude came from Tessenei in the western lowlands of Eritrea and joined me in Adi Ugri. John and I agreed that I should use the sitting room as my bedroom and John used the other bedroom. If we had visitors, my bedroom was our sitting room. In that second year, we hired Yemane Russom as our houseboy, and he slept in a sleeping bag in the entrance hall at the front of the house.

Remnants of War

World War II was a distant memory to me, but in Eritrea I saw reminders of the war in 1962. The school where we taught had served as a prisoner of war camp twice in its history. The school first held Ethiopian prisoners during the Italian invasion of Ethiopia in 1935, and in 1941 the Italians were held there when the British took over Eritrea. Still looking like a prison in 1962, six long buildings lined a central walkway, and a chain link fence surrounded the former prison. The prison commandant's two-story house was home for the three Peace Corps "girls."

Ruins of a small airfield could still be seen east of Adi Ugri. It may have been built by the Italians before their invasion of Ethiopia in 1935, or maybe the British built it later during their occupation of Eritrea. The buildings were gone, but the gravel runways were easy to see.

An aerial tramway once rose from Massawa on the Eritrean coast on the Red Sea to the mountains at Asmara. Cables strung between tall steel towers had carried cargo on overhead pulleys up from the harbor at Massawa. The aerial tramway could deliver supplies to Asmara more quickly than trucks on the winding roads below. In the early 1960s, the towers and cables still stood like silent reminders of the war.

The Second World War lingered in the minds of older Eritreans. One day I was on my way to the Adi Ugri post office, when an old Eritrean woman stopped me and pleaded with me in Tigrinya. She was asking for something, but I couldn't understand her. A helpful man heard her and explained.

"Her husband was in the Italian army," he explained. "He died, and she thinks you are an Italian. She thinks she should have a widow's income, and she wants you to pay her."

I don't remember, but I hope I gave her some money.

JOURNEY TO ETHIOPIA: 1962-1964

Lete Dehab Habut

Water, Cooking, Bathing, and Laundry in Adi Ugri

Bill Kerske (and later John Rude) and I couldn't have lived in Adi Ugri had it not been for our maid, Lete Dehab Habut. Lete (Leh-tay) will appear in several places in this book, so you need to meet her now. Lete was a war widow whose husband had died in the Italian army that resisted the British invasion of Eritrea in 1941. Life had not been kind to her. She was only about 42 when I met her, but she could have passed for sixty. Lete cooked for Bill and me, and later for John and me, in the back yard at the boys' house. She used a round concrete pedestal as her food preparation table. It may have been created for outdoor cooking.

Iob (E-ohb) Araia, our Headmaster, knew that Bill and I couldn't teach school full time and also do our own cleaning, shopping, and cooking so he brought a shy Eritrean woman to our house. Iob's endorsement was enough for us, and we hired Lete.

"Lete" is a title rather than a name. It means "servant." Her full name was Lete Dehab Habut, and she hovered over Bill Kerske and me more like a mother hen. She was our "Mama Dehab," our Adi Ugri mama, and she loved that title.

Lete was born in 1920, so she was forty-two years old in 1962 when we hired her. She was the widow of an Eritrean soldier who fought for the Italians and had been killed at the Battle of Keren during the British invasion of Eritrea in 1941. Lete was a devout Orthodox Christian, and her one-room apartment was in the very shadow of the main Adi Ugri church. She slept on a thin mattress on a raised part of the clay floor, and she went to church very early in the morning before she came to our house.

Lete was a stocky woman who wore ankle-length dresses, usually made of floral print cloth. She wore her hair in tightly braided "corn rows" except for a little knot of hair at the back that formed a tuft just above her collar line. She once came to our house with her hair unbraided, and we saw a larger mass of hair than we expected. She came to our house with unbraided hair only once or twice in two years.

Each morning, Lete came to our house with a pan of burning charcoal that she used to start a fire. She first made her excellent coffee, and when Bill and I were dressed, she placed coffee and scrambled eggs on the table. On some days we chose to have imported cold cereal. After breakfast, we were off to school.

Lete must have cooked scrambled eggs for Italians, because hers were not leathery and overcooked like the ones we had at the University College in Addis Ababa.

We bought several cheap aluminum cooking pans and had no place to store them. We bought a peg board and mounted it on a wall in the kitchen, and we hung our handle-less pans on the board. We called the board of pans "Lete's Control Panel." When she had washed the pans she had used for a meal, she sometimes stood in front of the Control Panel for several minutes trying to remember where each pan went.

The "boys' house" in Adi Ugri had running water and overnight electricity. Running water came from a concrete reservoir that sat high on a hill above the town. The water was pumped up to the reservoir from a well, and then flowed by gravity from the reservoir to homes like ours. A spigot supplied water to an outdoor sink and to a sink in a bathroom building attached to the house. There was no running water in the house itself.

The bathroom building at the boys' house had a Western style sit-down toilet and a sink with running water. The city water was unsafe for drinking or even for brushing teeth and shaving, so we asked Lete to boil our water for 30 minutes before using it. Water boils at a lower temperature at high altitude, but boiling our water for 30 minutes must have been enough to kill amoeba and other germs. We were healthy nearly all the time. We men each used a cup of boiled water when we brushed our teeth, but we were careful not to rinse our toothbrushes in the tap water in our lean-to bathroom. We even took boiled water from the kitchen out to the bathroom for shaves every few days.

A shallow basin in the bathroom building's concrete floor was intended for showers. A two-inch drain hole in the basin was fitted with a wooden plug to keep rats from climbing up out of the sewer and into the bathroom. There was a showerhead, but only cold tap water came from it, so we took baths instead of showers. The dry, thin air in Adi Ugri kept body odor low so we didn't take baths every day.

Bill Kerske and I bought a soft, blue, plastic bathtub barely large enough to hold one of us at a time. About twice each week, Lete heated enough water for baths on the charcoal stove in the back yard. We took turns carrying the hot water into the bathroom building and pouring it into the blue plastic bathtub. After each bath, we would pull the wooden plug from the floor basin and pour the bath water down the hole in the floor. We always put the plug back in the hole to keep sewer rats from climbing out. (I never asked about the town's sewage system and where the water and waste went.)

Rats were common in the sewers and elsewhere One day I was told of a policeman in Adi Ugri who had a deathly fear of rats He was arresting a man for urinating in the street, and the man yelled, "Rat!" The policeman fainted from fear, and the man he was arresting beat him up and ran away. The "girls' house" on the school compound had a "squatty potty," sometimes called a Turkish toilet, plus a shower. The toilet was recessed into the floor, not raised with a seat like Western toilets, and there were raised places in the toilet's basin for your feet. To use the squatty potty, you would put your feet on the raised spaces in the shallow toilet basin and crouch over it. It took some practice, but we all learned how to use that kind of toilet. The girls' shower had only cold running water, so they rarely used it and bathed with heated water somewhere in the house. I don't know where and how the girls bathed.

The Peace Corps girls and boys in Adi Ugri lived separate lives, but we got together socially and sometimes joked about the possibility of romantic attractions between the boys and the girls. A popular song in the States at that time was "My Baby Does the Hanky Panky," so we developed our own version:

> I went to the girls' house to get a cup of tea,
> I looked into the window, and what did I see?
> Hanky panky! Hanky panky going on!

The song itself was enough to suppress romantic impulses.

One time while the three women PCVs were visiting Bill and me at the boys' house, we began clowning about the blue bathtub. We made a tape recording of our hysterical laughter, but the recording has been lost.

I have referred to the three Adi Ugri Peace Corps women as "girls," because that was what we called them then. They called the Peace Corps men "boys." We were all in our early twenties and single, so it made sense.

Food and Drink

It wouldn't have been Ethiopia without its distinctive foods and drinks. Ethiopian food and beverages were served with hospitality that could be elaborate and almost biblical. The most distinct flavor in Ethiopian cooking comes from a red-hot pepper mix called "berbere." (You may hear it pronounced "berry berry" like the thiamin-deficiency disease beriberi, but there's no relationship.) When the famous Ethiopian meat dish is fully seasoned, it is so hot it will burn your mouth and make you sweat. The aroma of Ethiopian food is as distinct as its flavor. If you are around Ethiopian cooking, the fragrance of berbere overcomes all other smells. During the Korean War, British soldiers camped near Ethiopian solders could always tell when the Ethiopian soldiers were cooking.

Wat is Amharic for the spicy Ethiopian meat sauce. *Wat* is pronounced with a popping "t" at the end. To make the pronunciation clear, it's sometimes written with a capital T at the end; *waT*. *Zigini* is the Tigrinya name for the hot meat sauce. *Injera*, the thin, pancake-like sourdough bread, offsets the burning heat of the meat sauce. *Wat* and *injera* are eaten with your fingers, not with a fork or spoon, so it's customary for the host to provide soap and water for washing before eating.

At a traditional Ethiopian meal, three or four large, round *injeras* are laid flat on a round serving tray about three feet across. Meat sauce and vegetables are poured in the middle, and you tear off pieces of *injera* for lifting the food to your mouth. You lay a piece of *injera* on the sauce and press down to pick up pieces of meat and vegetables. Boiled eggs are usually part of this meal, and you can crush an egg with your *injera* and eat it with the sauce.

Making *injera* is a science I know only from seeing Lete make it. Flour for injera is made from Teff (popping "T") grain, a tiny, shiny grain a little larger than grass seed. In the fields, Teff looks like overgrown lawn grass that has gone to seed. Teff is ground into flour and mixed with water to form the thin *injera* batter, which can be nearly as white as pancake batter, tan, or light gray. Most *injera* is tan or light gray.

Lete Dehab Habut making an injera.

The *injera* batter is allowed to ferment for three days before it's cooked on a large, round, stoneware griddle. The griddle is heated over a small fire and lightly oiled before the batter is poured on. Lete would start pouring at the outer edge and make a spiral of injera batter to the center of the stone. She would cover the *injera* with a basket-like lid while the injera was cooking. She slid a flat woven grass pad under the finished injera to lift it to a large serving tray. She repeated the process until she had a stack of *injeras* or until the batter was gone.

Injera griddles were made by women at a village between Adi Ugri and Asmara. At the bus stop, a woman would load one or two finished injera griddles onto the bus and ride with them into Asmara to be sold.

Lasagna

Lasagna is an Italian dish, but I had my first dose of it at the Bella Vista Hotel in Adi Ugri. (Bella Vista means "beautiful view.")

The Bella Vista Hotel and the local prison in Adi Ugri were both on a hill across the road from the boys' house. The owner of the Bella Vista, Señor Bosi, was also the main cook. He was a friendly Italian who spoke French and a few words of English in addition to his native Italian. By 1962, the Bella Vista had seen better days, but it was still the best hotel in town with the best Italian food. The hotel cast its spell over Adi Ugri when Señor Bosi played Italian opera on his record player. The enchanting sound of opera drifted down to our house if the wind was from the west.

The other Peace Corps volunteers had lasagna before and were glad to learn that Señor Bosi could cook it. I was in for a treat. The lasagna that first evening may have been three inches tall. Tomato sauce oozed through layers of pasta, melted cheese, Italian sausage, and Italian spices. After that night, I often ordered lasagna at Asmara restaurants.

Many years later, my wife Darlene made lasagna that was as good as Señor Bosi's. I used Darlene's recipe to make lasagna for guests or for church dinners, but no one ever said that my lasagna was good as Señor Bosi's or Darlene's.

Eritrean Tea and *Ful*

Eritrean tea was served in private homes, and there were also lots of tea houses in every town. The tea was boiled with sugar and cloves in blue enamelware teapots and served in tiny glass cups without handles that you picked up with a finger and thumb on opposite sides of the rim.

JOURNEY TO ETHIOPIA: 1962-1964

One special tea house in Adi Ugri was the *"ful bet"* (pronounced "fool bate"), or the *ful* house. *Ful* is a bean mash served in clarified butter. The flavor was mild unless you added a pinch of *beriberi* or chopped onion, as most local people did. *Ful* was eaten by breaking off pieces of a hard-crusted Italian roll, dipping the bread into the *ful,* and popping bite after bite into your mouth.

At the *ful bet,* a ragged kid about eight years old took orders and yelled dramatically to the cook in back, *"Wahed shayee* ('one tea'), *shahan ful!* ('dish of *ful')".* He brought a tray of tiny tea glasses and a pot of tea. In a moment he was back with bowls of *ful* and a basket of hard Italian rolls. The boy's energy and the *ful* launched you into your day, whatever the day might hold.

Years after I had left Eritrea, I longed for a bowl of ful, so I called my friend Isaac in Asmara for the recipe. I wrote the recipe as he spoke, and I made it at home in Wisconsin to satisfy my craving. I haven't made it for many years, but maybe tomorrow will be the day for ful.

Coffee

Ethiopia is the "Mother of all Coffee," it's safe to say. It came originally from Kaffa Province in southwestern Ethiopia, so the name is possibly a link to the origin of the word *coffee.* An early traveler may have thought the hot, black drink was called "Kaffa" when in fact he was being told where the beans had been harvested. Foreigners began to call it *kaffe, café, coffee*, and similar names. By contrast in Ethiopia, where coffee's real name and origin are known, coffee is called "bun" or "bunna." (It's too late to correct that ancient mistake.)

Ethiopian coffee is served in tiny Arabian cups that hold about a fourth of a cup of liquid. If you go to an Ethiopian restaurant to try the coffee, it will be served in the little cups with no handles, so you must grasp your cup rim with your fingertips and thumb in the same way that you hold the little glass teacups. Your reward will be a flavorful sip of some of the strongest coffee you are likely to taste anywhere.

Coffee cups

Some of the coffee I drank in Eritrea was brewed in a clay flask called a *"jebenah"*. A *jebenah* is shaped like the glass beakers you may have used in a chemistry class. It is round at the bottom with a six-inch stem for pouring the coffee. It has a pottery handle on one side so it can be picked up for pouring. I had grown up in Ohio and had learned to drink mild Folger's coffee thinned out with milk and sweetened with sugar, the way my parents drank it. In Adi Ugri, I began to drink very strong coffee, the kind Lete made. I could never go back to the weak version of America coffee.

Lete made our coffee from green Ethiopian coffee beans that she bought in the Adi Ugri market. She roasted the beans in our back yard in a frying pan over a charcoal fire, and a heavenly aroma floated over the house. After roasting the beans, she poured them into a steel tube that looked like the base of a military mortar shell. She ground the beans by plunging a steel rod into them in the tube.

After pounding the coffee beans, she boiled the coffee in a clay *jebenah* flask. A wad of horsehair in the stem of the *jebenah* filtered the coffee to keep large pieces of coffee grounds out of the cup when pouring.

Although it was a special treat to have our coffee made in the jebinah, Lete usually made coffee by a drip method, pouring boiling water over coffee grounds in the upper portion of a two-chamber Italian metal pot. That coffee was strong, and it could keep me awake on the drowsiest afternoon.

Illegal Charcoal

The coffee that Lete prepared for us couldn't have been brewed without the charcoal she used for cooking. Her little cooking stove was made from the bottom half of a four-liter (one gallon) petrol can. She adjusted the burning pieces of charcoal with her calloused fingers and snapped an index finger against a middle finger each time she handled the burning coals. I never tried to pick up burning charcoal with my bare hands like Lete. She was much tougher than I was.

Buying charcoal was not as simple as going to the local hardware or grocery store for it. Charcoal had been made illegal to try to allow newly planted eucalyptus trees to grow on the hillsides near Adi Ugri, so buying charcoal had become a secretive activity. Every month or two after dark, someone would knock on our gate. It was the charcoal man, coming at night because he made his charcoal illegally.

The charcoal didn't come in tidy lumps like you find in your local store now. Instead, it came in the shapes of the limbs the man had cut to make it. Somewhere out in the wild, he would build a stack of branches and cover the stack with dirt leaving small passages at the bottom of the pile and at the top for air to pass through. He would start a small fire at the bottom of this mound of dirt and branches, and the fire would drive out moisture and cook the branches into charcoal. We happily participated in the illegal trade.

Souwa, Mes, Talla, **and** *Tej*

Souwa and *Mes* are the Tigrinya names for drinks known in Amharic as *Talla* and *Tej*. These drinks are so ancient that they must have been present when the Queen of Sheba lived in Ethiopia, and they may be among the strong drinks that the Bible warns us about.

Talla is pronounced with a popping "T." It may be easier to call it *souwa*, its Tigrinya name. *Souwa* is a grain beverage like beer, but it's home-brewed and non-carbonated. It comes in a variety of colors from gray or brown to cream colored and almost white, depending on how it's made. Its alcohol content is about 5 percent, a little higher than American beers, and in Eritrea it's usually served in tall metal cups that hold nearly quart. You will find *souwa* houses in cities, towns, and tiny villages. *I drank souwa in remote villages, and its alcohol content may be the reason I didn't have dysentery.*

Tej, also pronounced with a popping "T," is a honey wine known in Tigrinya as *mes* ("mayse"), similar to what Europeans in early times called *mead*. Honey, water, yeast, and other ingredients are combined to create *Tej*, and it's fermented at room temperature for a week or two, the longer time being needed during cool weather. The alcohol content of *Tej* can vary from

5 percent to 15 percent or more, but the lower level is most common in Eritrea. I had *Talla* in villages and at weddings in Adi Ugri, but Tej was less common. I only remember having *Talla* few times at restaurants in Asmara.

Among Eritrean drinks, Italian beer should be mentioned. It's not native to Eritrea and some snobs might smirk at the mere mention of Italian beer. Melotti Beer was made in Asmara and was considered a good beer by the more knowledgeable Peace Corps people. It was brewed by Italians for Italians and for anyone else who wanted carbonated European beer. (Other brands of European beer and wine and hard liquor were available in Asmara stores, but I can't mention every form of worldliness here.)

Prickly Pears

Here we go round the prickly pear
Prickly pear prickly pear
Here we go round the prickly pear
At five o'clock in the morning.

From T.S. Eliot, "The Hollow Men"

Cactus pears, prickly pears, and bellus are various names for the fruit of a cactus that grows wild on hillsides in Eritrea. The oblong pear forms along the edges of flat cactus leaves, and inside each pear is the mass of seeds and soft, juicy fruit. You can slice open a prickly pear and eat the fruit, but the pear is covered with short, tiny needles that will stab your tender fingers if you do this without gloves.

Young Eritrean girls whose hands were toughened by hard farm work would go out on the mountainsides and pick burlap bags full of prickly pears with their bare hands. They'd take the pears to the streets of Asmara and sell them as sidewalk treats. The seller would slice open a prickly pear and pop the fruit safely, into the mouth of a customer. I was told you could become constipated eating too many, but I never ate enough to find out if that's true.

Eritrean cactus pears had a dramatic seasonal price cycle. When they were first ripe enough to eat, the price was high. As the season went on, the price dropped until one pear could be bought cheaply.

CHAPTER 7

ST. GEORGE SCHOOL

St. George School, where the Peace Corps teachers taught, was a mile south of Adi Ugri. Students came from the town itself, but also from farther away. Some of our boys from distant villages rented rooms in chilly stone buildings on the edge of the Adi Ugri market. They cooked together and studied under the town streetlights in the cold night air. Other students commuted on foot each day to their home villages, sometimes several kilometers each way.

Our school was itself a village of sorts, but its population oscillated over the course of a school day. During the day there were nearly 1,000 students and teachers on the property. At night only the three Peace Corps women were there with a *sabanya* (guard), his family, and two other families. An old warrior named Guadat was the campus *sabanya*. He was comforted on cold nights and chilly days by a heavy woolen military coat that may have dated from his time in the Italian-Eritrean army. At sundown he turned on the school's electric generator and kept the school's lights on until 11:00 p.m.

Meeting the Headmaster and Teachers

Our Headmaster at the St. George School was Ato Iob Araia. "Ato" means "Mister" in Tigrinya and Amharic, and it is used as a formal title. His first name, Iob, means "Job," and it had poetic meaning because he needed "the patience of Job" to fulfill his many roles as headmaster and as a leading figure in the community. He ran a school of over 1,000 students and 30 teachers, and he carefully choreographed our entry into Adi Ugri life, helping us meet people and get settled in our homes.

Ato Iob met us on the day we arrived, and he told us there would be a reception for us at the Teachers' Club across the street from the boys' house in town. On the evening of the reception, the girls came to town and all five of us trouped across the street to the meeting. Chairs had been set up for us at one end of a large rectangular room. The teachers were already seated around other sides of the room and were studying us closely.

Iob served as the master of ceremonies. He stood and greeted the Peace Corps teachers on behalf of the local teachers and the town of Adi Ugri. He asked each of the PCVs to tell where we were from in the States, a little about our families, and what we would teach. After they heard from us, he said the teachers could ask questions. One by one, we introduced ourselves as Iob had asked. I may have joked about being named "Nyle." I probably claimed that the Nile River is named for me, and they may have smiled to please me.

Iob then invited the Eritrean teachers to ask questions. There was an awkward silence. Finally, a round-faced man at the far end of the room stood.

"I have seen American films at the cinema," he said. "Here is what I want to know. Why do the Red Indians have no beards?"

No one laughed or even smiled. Other teachers must have wondered the same thing, since beards and moustaches were so common among Eritrean men. We Peace Corps teachers wondered too, and I offered an answer.

"I think the American Indian men can't grow beards like white men, and the few hairs of their faces are pulled out when they are young. The hair doesn't grow back." (To this day, I don't know if American Indians have beards and if not, why not.)

The man who asked about Native American facial hair was Isaac Joseph. He became my closest Eritrean friend.

Dr. Google offers answers to the question about Native Americans and their beards. Most of the entries insist that Native Americans can grow facial hair, but they also acknowledge that their facial hair tends to be sparse, thin, and soft. Their facial hair is similar to that of Asian men, and it's believed that Asians crossed a land bridge into North America and became Native American Indians.

Iob Araia Brings Lete

Headmaster Iob Araia was a fine man and a dapper dresser. He wore a suit and tie to school every day. His hair was cropped short, and he had an intelligent, kind face. He was in charge of our school, and he reported to the local school superintendent, Ato Saari. Iob had been a classroom teacher earlier in his career, and he may have run a small school before coming to St. George. Family connections may have helped him get his job, but he was a good man for the school, no matter how he got the job.

Iob had been working with the Peace Corps for a few months before we arrived. It was up to Iob to decide how he would use the Peace Corps teachers, the subjects we would teach, and where we would be housed.

Headmaster Iob Araia and his wife

On the day we arrived, Iob met us to check on our simple, unfinished furniture. He couldn't stay long because he had a full schedule that day, as always. Knowing we couldn't live at our houses without help, he came to the boys' house the next day with a maid named Lete. She seemed old, but she was only about forty. She spoke Tigrinya and some Amharic and Italian, but very little if any English. When we first met her, she was so shy she looked at the ground most of the time, only chancing glances up to see what her employers looked like.

Iob had divided the students at each grade level into sections and assigned them to classrooms. He gave each of us a few thin textbooks, a flexible curriculum outline, and the freedom to find our way as teachers. Having launched us, Iob left us to do our work with very little interference from him. For young teachers, it was a marvelous opportunity for independence as we learned how to teach.

Lete and the Houseboys

The jobs of cleaning, shopping, cooking, and tending charcoal fires were too much for one person, so Lete needed a helper, a houseboy. Our first houseboy was Umberto Bosi, a sociable, strong young man of about twenty. He was half Italian, what the Eritreans called a "half-caste." He had loosely curled dark hair, a milk chocolate complexion, and a bold but sociable style. Boys like Umberto who ran loose in the streets, were called "street boys." He must have been a leader among the street boys of Adi Ugri.

Lete had little respect for Umberto. She was a devout woman of faith, and he lived by his wits in the streets. She scolded him and argued with him so much that we eventually had to let him go to have peace in the house. Umberto may have met a tragic end during the civil war.

Fetui Ghebrejohannes was our next houseboy. He was a cute little guy, younger and smaller than Umberto, and he may have been only ten years old. He was a nice boy with a winning smile, but Lete tyrannized him too, so we had to let him go. Our next helper came near the beginning of the 1963–64 school year and lasted only a couple of weeks. This time the helper was a girl, and she was even younger than Fetui. Her name escapes me.

We finally hired Yemane Russom, our best helper. He came from a village named Adi Ghered, a short walk off the highway to Asmara. Ato Iob brought Yemane to us when he started at the school in September 1963, explaining that he was very poor and needed a job. *Yemane's story is told later.*

Soon after we hired Lete in 1962, I had to take her to Kagnew Station in Asmara for a chest X-ray to make sure she didn't have tuberculosis. We rode the bus together to Asmara, and the Peace Corps director loaned me a Peace Corps jeep for the drive into Kagnew Station. Lete was astounded to see that I could drive a car. It probably increased my status in her eyes.

Lete had no children, so I became her adoptive son. She called me *"Nyo weday,"* which meant, "Nyle, my son." She cared for me and protected me as though I were the son she never had.

Lete made a *shama* for me, a large piece of cloth that Ethiopians fold in a special way to wear on their shoulders. A *shama* is similar to a thick blanket sheet with two layers of soft cotton cloth. Lete used thick cotton yarn she made on a tiny hand-held spindle. She held the spindle in one hand and spun it between her thumb and fingers. There was a tiny hook at the end of the spindle to snag bits of cotton that she spun into thick yarn.

To hold the shama together, her weaver wove thin, white commercial thread across the strands of the thick yarn.

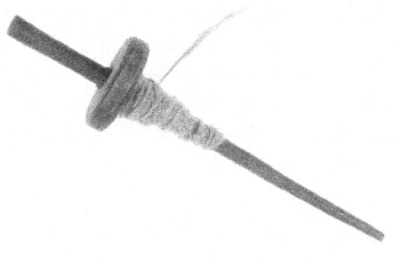

Cotton Spindle

One of the teachers at St. George School taught me how to wear a shama on ordinary days and on special occasions, like meeting a king. I still have Lete's shama, and I wear it on some winter evenings. A heavy shama is called a "gabi" ("ga-bee").

I sometimes tried to surprise Lete with antics I thought were entertaining, but she rarely laughed at my clowning. She often exclaimed, *"Wylekagado!"* It was Lete's way of saying, "Oh my goodness!" or something like it. My teasing sometimes wore thin and she would say, *"Kom-ui-te-geber!"* That was Lete's rebuke, and it meant, "Don't treat me that way!"

Lete didn't laugh when Mr. Sipe, an old American visitor, ate his lunch in our living room one day. He was an agricultural extension agent for the Agency for International Development. He brought his American-style lunch whenever he came, and on this visit Mr. Sipe's lunch included a can of Vienna sausages, sausages that look like tiny hot dogs. On this particular day, Lete came to clean up the room where Mr. Sipe and I had eaten our lunches. She quickly gathered up his napkin and empty containers and surveyed the floor. Spotting something on the floor, she said to herself, *"Enty zi?"* ("What is this?") and picked up a Vienna sausage.

"Weyle kegado!" she screamed and threw the tiny sausage on the floor. I could tell what she thought the sausage was. It took me a minute to stop laughing.

On a more spiritual level, Bill Kerske brought Lete a bottle of water he had dipped from the Jordan River during our visit there in summer 1963. He thought she might have herself anointed with it, but to her the water was holy, so she drank it—all of it.

Poor as she was, Lete practiced Christian charity by giving some of our table scraps and some of her very limited money to a beggar woman who sat on the curb opposite our gate nearly every day.

The woman chanted, *"Selez getinna Mariam!"* I think that was a plea for donations in the name of Mary. We sometimes gave her money, and Lete probably fed her some of her food as well as some of ours. I think the beggar lady joined Lete in heaven many years ago.

Begging was common, especially in Asmara and Addis Ababa, so I needed a policy about beggars. Most beggars probably were in desperate conditions, but some simply begged because it was easier than working or was their form of work. I couldn't tell which ones were in the greatest need, so I gave just a little money to almost every beggar who asked.

The Adi Ugri Five

Bill Kerske, a history major from California, taught history and English grammar. Gloria Somple had graduated from the Indiana State College of Indiana, Pennsylvania (a school name she had to explain many times). She included poetry and literature in her English teaching, and she taught art after school. Cynthia Tse, a liberal arts major from San Francisco, taught science with emphasis on astronomy and the solar system. Jackie Woodson, from the University of Washington, taught English and world history. I had graduated from Anderson College with a major in math and a minor in education. I taught science the first year and geometry the second year.

The five Peace Corps teachers were an unusual sight at the school and in town, and there must have been a lot of talk about us. Bill Kerske had red hair and a fair complexion, and he was a little rounded physically. I was a skinny paleface with brown hair. Cynthia Tse was of Chinese origin and may have been the first Chinese person most people in Adi Ugri had ever seen. Jackie Woodson was a tall, muscular brunette, and Gloria Somple was a slim, fast-talking blonde. We were quite a spectacle.

Most of the teachers had bicycles, but most students walked to and from the school on a wide, eucalyptus-lined path beside the road. Each of the Peace Corps teachers had been issued a heavy Italian-made bicycle with a sturdy luggage rack above the rear fender. Bill Kerske and I tied our books to our racks for the ride to school each morning.

Bill and I were conspicuous as we rode our bikes a mile out of town to the school. We rode our bikes on the tarmac, dodging herds of sheep, goats, and cattle. The road from town to the school was shared by occasional trucks, cars, and buses, but the most picturesque were cattle, sheep, and goats being driven along the same road.

The Peace Corps "girls" only had to cross the school grounds to walk to class.

At the end of the 1962–63 school year Bill, Cynthia, and Jackie left for other schools in Ethiopia, and Jody Donovan, Katie Schultz, and John Rude came to replace them. Jody was trained in science and went on to a career in medical technology. Katie Schutz was an English teacher in Adi Ugri and in the states later. John Rude had been in the western lowland town of Tessenei

JOURNEY TO ETHIOPIA: 1962-1964

the first year and was happy to teach English in the cooler climate of Adi Ugri. Gloria and I stayed in Adi Ugri for two years.

Gloria Somple made a strong impression on her students with her English teaching and her artwork, and one of them composed a song about her.

In praise of her good work and her love for them. This phrase was repeated in the song:

> *Somple-a-awayna!*
>
> *Somple-a-awayna!*

Jackie Woodson had learned some rounds in her camping life in the Pacific Northwest. She led us in singing rounds (the only "round" I had sung before was "Row, Row, Row Your Boat"). Jackie introduced us to "All Is Silent," "Joan Come Kiss Me Now," "Go to Joan Glover," and "Marching to Pretoria." Here are the words for "All Is Silent."

> *All is silent, nightingale only,*
>
> *Lures with the sweetest, softest music,*
>
> *Tears to the eyes and joys to the heart.*

The words were repeated as the second and third voices joined. It was a beautiful sound.

Gloria Somple was already engaged when she joined the Peace Corps. She and her fiancé, Charles Perrino, met in Rome in summer 1964 and married there. Gloria raised a family and continues her artwork in California now.

Cynthia Tse Kimberlin taught herself to play the guitar at Adi Ugri and began collecting Ethiopian songs. She is a widely recognized ethnomusicologist specializing in Ethiopian music.

Bill Kerske went directly from the Peace Corps to Boalt Hall, the law school at the University of California, Berkeley. He became an attorney for Coca-Cola before his untimely death in 1992.

Jackie Woodson went to a town in southern Ethiopia for her second year. She studied history at the University of Washington after her return. Jackie died in about 2012.

CBS Comes to Adi Ugri

Our lives in school were shared with the world when a camera crew from CBS came to Adi Ugri to tape a program for American TV. The best account of that day is from PCV Gloria (Semple) Perrino's diary from that time. The following is Gloria Perrino's diary entry she shared with me by email on March 22, 2022.

Bill Canby, the Eritrea Peace Corps Director, came on Tuesday, November 6, 1962, to tell us that CBS would visit in the next day or two. They showed up on Thursday with Canby. Two of the men worked out of London, one was from Paris and Harry was from New York. They took shots all over Ethiopia the previous four weeks. We were the only Peace Corps Volunteers they took. The footage was to be used for a show called "The 20th Century with Walter Cronkite" in February or March of the following year.

They filmed us walking home from school with the students, buying vegetables downtown at the market, Cynthia teaching Science, and a group discussion with Blaine, the interviewer. He asked questions about what, if any, problems we're facing; what we came to Ethiopia for; how we liked our experience thus far.

The show will last 30 minutes, and they shot about ten hours of film in Ethiopia. We will be on for about three minutes.

CBS Cameraman at St. George School.

They bought us lunch at the hotel--spaghetti, salad, chicken--delicious. They stayed at school all afternoon, took film of us jumping rope with the students.

In my only comment during the interview, I said that the value to us Peace Corps teachers probably would be greater than any good we could do for our students. My comment didn't make it into the program. One of the others mentioned the kite I had made for the kids, and that didn't make it into the program. Still, it was exciting to know we had been on American TV.

Teaching

"Memhir" is the Tigrinya word for "teacher." Teachers in Eritrea had higher status than in the United States, so Peace Corps teachers had to learn to live with their high status and their visibility. We were in Ethiopia to teach and advance civilization, but some of us wished that we could just explore Eritrea and get to know its people.

On our first day of school, we walked to school surrounded by crowds of students. Headmaster Iob Araia took us from classroom to classroom, introducing us. When we entered, the students leapt to their feet and stood at attention when we entered. It was their traditional show of respect. This was different from the casual glance a visitor might have gotten from students in an American classroom.

In the 1962–63 school year, the school went only through eighth grade, and our assignments were in grades 6, 7, and 8. I taught science to 6th, 7th, and 8th grade students, a subject our Headmaster called "sinus." The British science textbook was only about a quarter of an inch thick, and I added experiments my students could understand. Following are a few examples of my science lessons.

- The Barometer: The British science textbook described a mercury barometer, so I bought some mercury in Asmara for a barometer. I put a thin glass tube into a small container of mercury, and melted the top of the glass tube shut with a Bunsen burner. When the air in the heated tube cooled, it drew the mercury up to create a tall column of mercury. We could then see the mercury rise and fall in the tube when the air pressure went up or down. Luckily, it rained the next day out of season, and the mercury dropped as if predicting the rain and I was an instant celebrity scientist. (Later I learned that the Tigrinya word for "rain" is *"zenab." Zenab y'zem balu* means "it is raining" or "the rain it is raining." To say that it is going to rain, they say, *"Zenab k'metsiu,"* translated "rain it is coming.")

- Falling Objects: The science textbook told of Galileo's claim that a feather and stone will fall at the same rate, in a vacuum. I tried to demonstrate this principle of gravity with two rocks of different sizes. I climbed to the top of the school's water tower and pushed two stones from the top. The two stones appeared to land at the same time, though neither was light as a feather, and they weren't falling in a vacuum. Galileo's fame increased at the St. George School and the students were impressed.

- Vinegar and Baking Soda: In another experiment, I poured baking soda into a glass bottle and added vinegar. The expanding carbon dioxide gas blew the cork off the bottle. The point of the experiment must have been something about chemistry. It was one of my more dramatic moments in the classroom.

- The Solar System: You can't actually do experiments on the sun and its planets, but in a lesson on the solar system, I used a ball of cord to demonstrate the distances from the sun to three of the sun's closest planets. With the students' help, we strung cord across the school's gravel parade ground. By choosing the right units of measurement, we could see that the solar system is really big. We could estimate that the more remote planets would be a couple of villages away, but we didn't have enough string to prove it.

Bill, Gloria, Cynthia, and Jackie held night classes in English for adults at a room in downtown Adi Ugri. Gloria taught an art class and a cooking class for girls in the house at the school.

I taught a gymnastics class on the school grounds using woven grass mats to keep us out of the dust when we did handsprings and backward somersaults. The grass mats were not padded mats filled with grass; they were simply made of grass woven into mats, and they were very thin. They just kept us out of the dust and pebbles.

School began at 9 a.m., and there was a lunch break from 12:00 noon until 2:30 p.m. The long break gave teachers and students time to eat lunch and rest at school or go into town to cook and eat. Classes changed every 45 minutes when a hand bell was rung outside the buildings, and the teachers moved from room to room while the students stayed in their rooms. There were short morning and afternoon breaks and classes continued until 5:00 p.m., and everyone went home under a lowering sun. Sunset came at about 6:00 p.m. all year because we were near the equator.

Our classrooms were more highly regimented than the schools where we PCVs had grown up in in the U.S. At the St. George School students sat in rows of wide desks, two or three students to a desk. Desks along the side and back walls faced the center of the room, and one column of desks was in the middle of the room.

If a student arrived late for class, he or she tapped on the door and waited. When the teacher opened the door, the student said, *"Frakhad?"* ("Permission?") When permission was granted, the student slipped in, and class continued.

The classrooms were about 20 feet square, or 400 square feet, and there were about forty students in each classroom. In the 1962–63 year, the students in one of my seventh grade science classes were twelve to sixteen years old.

The blackboards in all the rooms were sheets of plywood that were painted with special black paint. They worked surprisingly well. I used my blackboard heavily, especially in the second year, when I taught plane geometry.

Our students showed the Eritrean racial mixture. Some students had light complexions that may have come from an Italian parent or grandparent. The lighter-skinned students were sometimes called "half-castes" if their features were light enough, or they might be called "café latte" – coffee with milk. Most of the students' skin was the color of dark chocolate.

If there was a disturbance in the class, I would ask who made the noise. A student might report, "It was the black one!"

"Which black one?" I wondered, because they all looked black to me.

Many of the students had facial features more Caucasian than mine. Those students had narrow, finely sculpted noses, and high cheekbones that accented their faces, possibly because Eritreans had mingled with Middle Eastern peoples from the east side of the Red Sea. My skin was light, but my nostrils were wider than those of some of the students, and my lips were wider than theirs. The rich mixture of features and colors made my students a very attractive bunch of kids.

Boredom in Paradise

Boredom set in after a few weeks of school. There were long pauses in the teaching day while students completed assignments in class, and I felt bored while waiting. I often gazed to the west through an open window while the students worked. A purple and gray mountain raised its head into the sky far off to the west. It seemed to call me to explore my new country.

One day my gazing toward the road paid off. We had heard that Zhou en Lai, the Premier of Communist China, was in Ethiopia and would travel north by motorcade past the school on his way from Ethiopia to Asmara. My classroom window faced the road, and I happened to look up just as the motorcade sped by.

I don't know how I could have been bored or lonely in Ethiopia. We were surrounded by interesting people and there were animals, food, and amazing geography and events all around us. I was typing a letter to my parents one day and began to tell them how peaceful life was in Eritrea. As I was writing, I remembered a terrible incident a few days earlier when rebels in the lowlands had thrown hand grenades into a truckload of Ethiopian soldiers, killing several men. I changed the tone of my letter and told my parents about that killing and other things that made life in Eritrea unpredictable and sometimes dangerous.

One day in the second year, I complained to John Rude that our teaching was keeping us from having adventures.

"*This is* an adventure!" John exclaimed.

I thought, "You might call it an adventure, but to me it seems routine."

John was right. We were having a greater adventure than I realized. We were committed to teaching and its daily routine, and I had lost perspective on the interesting, surprising things that happened often.

It may have been about November 1962 when I was shocked to realize, I was going to be there for two years.

Other Peace Corps teachers in Adi Ugri had had the same experience, and "Two Years!" became a byword for us. We usually said it when we felt our lives would go on for two years with one day following the last one without change.

We sometimes wished we could simply explore Eritrea rather than being tied to our teaching duties. Some of us wanted to "pull a Thoreau," referring to Henry David Thoreau's self-imposed isolation at Walden Pond. We were learning more than we realized, just by being there with our eyes and ears open.

Abunawas the School Teacher

I read this story in a small book of Tigrinya folk tales.

Abunawas is a mythical figure in Tigrinya or Amharic folk tales. He was an impish character who reminded me of stories I'd read about Till Eulenspiegel, a trickster in German literature who was hanged for his merry pranks.

Abunawas became a substitute teacher at a fictional school when no one else was available, but he really knew nothing to teach the kids. On the first day he went to class, he asked his students, "Who knows everything I'm going to teach you today?"

The students didn't know what he was going to teach them, so none of them raised their hands.

"Since you don't know anything, I have no place to start," said Abunawas, and he went to town to drink tea.

The next day, Abunawas came and asked the same question, "Who knows what I'm going to teach you today?"

They all raised their hands. "Well, you don't need me, since you know everything," he said and went to town again to drink tea.

On the third day, Abunawas returned. The students knew what to expect, so they conspired against him.

"Who knows what I'm going to teach you today?" Abunawas asked. Half the kids raised their hands, and the other half didn't.

"Okay!" said Abunawas, "Those who know, teach those who don't know," and *he went to town and spent the day drinking tea.*

Rediscovering English, the World's Language

I had lived in the United States until I was twenty-two, and my only samplings of languages other than English had been in church, where some of the older people prayed in German, and at home, where we lived next door to Spanish-speaking farm workers. I had also studied French in college. I didn't know that English is the world's most widely spoken language when you count people for whom English is a second or third language.

Before I lived in Ethiopia, I didn't know there were so many accents and dialects in English around the world. I knew of the Southern and Western accents in the U.S., and I knew that the Hispanic migrant workers from Texas had a special accent, but I didn't know of the accents of English speakers in Africa, Asia, and elsewhere.

We Peace Corps teachers naturally thought our version of English was normal, and we thought we could easily communicate in it. We soon learned that we needed to speak slowly, clearly, and distinctly, and we learned how "lazy mouthed" we could be with fellow English speakers. To make ourselves more easily understood by our students, we learned to exaggerate our enunciation and use smaller, more familiar words the students were likely to know. That made it easier for them to understand "our" English.

Still, they didn't always understand us. One day, in 1962, a student raised his hand and I called on him. He stood to speak.

"Sir," he said, "we do not understand your pronounce-ation!"

After his comment, I tried to speak more clearly than I ever had before.

Haile Ghebremusie was an especially bright Class 9 student, and he was curious about English. One day, he said to me, "Teach me some slangs."

I don't know how he knew of slang, but he must have sensed the fun and power in it. I suggested a few useful "slangs" to Haile but I didn't teach him any of the off-color English words.

The words *better* and *water* were especially difficult for our students. We Americans say those words with a flip of the tongue rather than by saying the letter "r" clearly the way a British person might. Our students tended to say "betterrr," and "waterrr."

Haile Ghebremusie worked hard to say "better" and "water" like an American, but it was hard, even for him.

Eritreans, and probably most Ethiopians, have difficulty with the "th" sound in English words such as *this, that,* and *those.* There is no "th" sound in Amharic or Tigrinya, and maybe not in the other languages in Ethiopia. It is easier for a Tigrinya speaker to make the "z" sound so the "th" words like *this, that,* and *those* become "zis," "zat," and "zose." It's a workable solution to a problem created by the English language.

Even for the brightest and bravest kids, it was a challenge to sound like an American or a Brit, but some of our students rose to the challenge of saying the "th" words like Americans. With practice, a student could press his tongue against his top front teeth for the "th" sound. If we hadn't gone to Ethiopia, we Peace Corps people wouldn't have known we had learned a special skill at a an early age. We could say "this" and "that" before we went to school.

We had to learn to understand the way English was used in Eritrea. Where English is the second or third language, it is adapted to the ways of speaking the people's first languages. For example, an Eritrean might ask "How are you?" by saying politely, "What is the condition of your body?" Asking in that way is perfectly correct; it's just not how we would ask in our version of English.

You might want to try to ask your friends about the condition of their bodies and see what they say.

If Lete spoke any English, it was only her own version of it. We usually spoke with her in a combination of Tigrinya, Amharic, Italian, and English. Some of Lete's expressions sounded like English to me. She said, *"harrai"* in Tigrinya, and it sounded like "all right" in English. I took it to mean "okay," and that's what she did mean.

She also said *"e-okway,"* maybe thinking she was speaking English. I never found out if "e-okway" meant something in Tigrinya, but I assumed it meant "okay." Maybe she was just speaking her version of English when she said it.

Americans often fail to learn languages other than English. We live in a large country where English is the national language, and English is spoken so widely around the world that American travelers can usually find English speakers wherever we go. At a hotel in Paris, I used some of my college French when trying to speak with the hotel's owner. She humored me through a few sentences of my awkward French and finally said in clear, unaccented English, "Maybe it will be best if we both speak English." And that's what we did.

Tigrinya, "My Mother's Tongue"

One of my students, explaining what Tigrinya meant to him, said, "Tigrinya is my mother's tongue."

The Peace Corps had been invited to Ethiopia by the ruling regime whose members spoke Amharic, the official national language. Amharic worked well for the volunteers farther south in Ethiopia, but in Eritrea, Amharic was a foreign language, and it sometimes wasn't welcome. Amharic was taught as a subject in Eritrean schools, but it was seen as the language of an oppressive power.

Speaking a few phrases of Amharic didn't help us make friends in Eritrea as well as speaking Tigrinya would have. To our untrained ears, Tigrinya sounded harsh. There are consonants that include clicks, pops, and guttural sounds formed deep in the throat. There are several variations on the "h" and "k" sounds that range from a soft "h" to a popping "k" to a deep, guttural "k" that I can't imitate in writing.

To Eritrean children, English seemed to be full of vowels, and it seemed to have a sing-song sound. In villages, children would mimic the sing-song way we seemed to speak. They would say something like *"Wayo weeya woyo!"* thinking they were speaking English.

A few of the Eritrean Peace Corps teachers were glad when we heard that Tigrinya classes would be offered in Asmara in the summer of 1963. Our instructor was Musa Aaron, a teacher from an evangelical school in Asmara. He began by teaching us the Tigrinya alphabet, which is the same as the Amharic alphabet. It's made up of syllables in which consonants form the base of each syllable and vowel sounds are attached to complete the sound. Musa Aaron also introduced us to Tigrinya greetings and phrases.

Suddenly the sounds we had been hearing began to make sense. The language that had sounded harsh began to sound beautiful.

The second year Peace Corps volunteers who joined us in 1963 had Tigrinya lessons during their training in the States. A volunteer named Ken Hatcher came in the second group, and I saw him at the Asmara bus station speaking Tigrinya confidently with everyone. People responded respectfully, so he must have been speaking Tigrinya correctly. I couldn't tell; I didn't know enough Tigrinya.

If you sneeze loudly and startle an Eritrean, he might say, *"K'mfizserer,"* meaning "Go ride a porcupine!" It meant that the speaker thought the sneeze was caused by excess internal air pressure that could have been released by riding on a porcupine and being punctured by its quills, releasing the air pressure quietly. The annoyed sneezer could say, *"Nehseccha Tay'kay!"* meaning "Then you will be my saddle!" to answer the insult.

Shemagelay is Tigrinya for "old wise person," a word I learned in Indianapolis from Harold Freeman, a second year PCV from Louisville, Kentucky. He and I went to an Eritrean Church festival in Indianapolis. At the meeting, Harold explained that we were *shemagelay,* old wise men, and we were given the courtesies reserved for *shemagelays* like us.

Lochmatz is a word you should use only very carefully, if at all. It means "liar." It was one of the terms my students used when teasing each other. I don't think I ever managed to work *lochmatz* into a conversation, at least not a serious one, and it's a good thing I didn't.

Ethiopia has ninety-two languages. In addition, many foreign languages are spoken, including English, Italian, Arabic, and French. Tigrinya is so closely related to the Hebrew language that an Israeli linguist visited Eritrea and within a few weeks was able to read Tigrinya.

You would hear a sound like trilling on special occasions. The sound is a repeated "la-la-la-la-la" cheering that women did at Ethiopian weddings or if a famous person drove by. Making the sound is called "ululating," and it can sound musical when a hundred people do it at once. I may be part Ethiopian because my mother used to call us children home at mealtime by trilling. She made a sound like a police whistle by making a high-pitched note while blowing over her relaxed tongue.

Adi Ugri Sights and Sounds

Adi Ugri had a population of about 9,000 in 1962, and by Ethiopian standards it was a small city and quite modern. A traffic circle was the town's center, with the post office and police station on one side and a pharmacy on the other. The Saturday marketplace was a few steps from the circle.

The daily bike ride to school was an experience in itself. The fragrant eucalyptus trees along the road reminded us that we were far, far from home. On the west side of the road was a threshing floor like those you can read about in the Bible, and there was a slaughterhouse with three sections for each of the main local religions: Orthodox, Catholic, and Muslim. (Evangelicals and other Protestant Christians were free to eat any meat they could afford, no matter how the animals were butchered.)

Isaac, my good friend, was feeling a little sick one day, and I went with him to the corner pharmacy. He asked the owner, Debesai, to give him an injection for his illness. I don't remember hearing how he described his illness. Isaac rolled up his sleeve, and Debesai gave him a shot of something. It seemed to make Isaac feel better.

At the Adi Ugri open air market you could buy eggs, chicken, and fresh meat any day of the week. Tailors made custom-fit clothing on their treadle sewing machines on a porch overlooking the marketplace.

When I was near the end of my two years, I went to an Adi Ugri tailor for a set of Ethiopian trousers and shirt, but I quickly outgrew the outfit back in the States.

On the west side of town, the livestock market swarmed with people and animals every Saturday. From the boys' house we could hear the hum of people.

At the market you could buy a tall metal cup of Ethiopian *souwa*, a cloudy, light brown beer. The alcohol level in *sua* varied widely, and the alcohol sometimes made men feel so bold that they threatened each other with their walking sticks. I saw men under the influence shaking their walking sticks at each other, but I never saw one of the men land a blow. Waving the sticks must have been for dramatic effect.

Eritrea was an example of Muslims and Christians living together peacefully. Adherents of the two religions were respectful of each other's holidays, with Muslim shops open on Christian holidays and Christian shops open on Muslim holidays. If there was conflict between Muslim and Christian students at St. George School, I never knew about it. I never heard students say anything about "that Muslim" or "that Christian."

Orthodox Christians and Muslims don't eat pork, but I saw a small corral of pigs on the west side of Adi Ugri one day. The pigs must have been raised for foreigners, including the declining number of Eritrean Italians. The pigs may have been owned by a tolerant Italian.

The most obvious building in Adi Ugri was the modern Ethiopian Orthodox church, and it was the symbol of the town. It stood on a hill high above the main road, and its rounded white sanctuary and tall bell tower gleamed in the sun. Haile Selassie was said to have provided funds for the church.

A Catholic church and school stood across the town's valley from the Orthodox church.

A Swedish mission church on the east side of Adi Ugri was led by Pastor Berglund, a huge, genial Swedish Lutheran pastor. He delivered sermons in Tigrinya, and also in English when the Peace Corps teachers were at the service. His sermons were well-reasoned and urgent appeals for the faith. The church was a simple, one-room building like the church I had attended as a boy in Ohio, and the pattern of worship was similar. The Swedish Lutheran church ran a preschool during the week for some of the youngest kids in town.

One of the mosques in Adi Ugri was to the east of our house, and I could see its minaret tower from our kitchen window. I often looked up from my lunch on Fridays to see the muezzin calling people to prayer. The call from the mosques was commanding and beautiful, and it reminded me that Arabia was just across the Red Sea.

When I returned to visit Adi Ugri in 1994, the Coptic church and the main mosque both had public address systems to amplify their calls to prayer.

CHAPTER 8

TRAVELING TALES

Bible Times in Eritrea

LIVING IN ERITREA IN THE early 1960s sometimes seemed like living in Bible times. Many things could have happened two or three thousand years earlier. Like young David shepherding his herds, boys as young as six or seven sometimes directed cattle a thousand pounds heavier than themselves. A column of cattle would come slowly into town at sunset with a young boy shouting instructions from the rear.

To the east of Adi Ugri, I saw shepherds "watching over their flocks by day." The sheep were up on a hillside, and I could hear the shepherds yelling and trilling to their sheep and goats. When the wind was gentle, I heard one of the shepherds playing a flute in the distance, just as David would have done. Shepherds in Eritrea had low status, but out in the fields, they were free from men and alone with God.

Hyenas and other predators lived in the hills near Adi Ugri, just as in Israel in David's time. An Eritrean shepherd probably could have killed a giant like Goliath to protect his herds.

Oxen pulled wooden plows through fields, just as oxen did two thousand years earlier. The man driving the plow called to the oxen and snapped a whip over the animals' heads.

Planting Teff and other grains was done by a broadcast method as in the biblical Parable of the Sower, and grain must have fallen on good soil and bad, just as Jesus explained in that parable. Teff was harvested with a sickle by a man who squatted on the ground to cut handfuls of grain.

At the threshing floor on the way into Adi Ugri from the school, an ox was yoked to a pole that led him in a circle around the threshing floor. Bundles of grain-bearing straw were thrown onto the smooth threshing floor. As the ox walked, its hoofs trampled the grain and loosened the chaff from the heads of grain. The threshers threw the straw and chaff into the air so the wind could blow away the chaff. The grain was heavier than the straw, and it fell to the threshing floor where it was swept up for more

thorough cleaning later. That way of threshing reminded me of Psalm 1:4: "The ungodly ... are like the chaff which the wind driveth away." KJV

Frankincense was burned in homes and churches. It is made of the hardened sap of a bush that grows in Eritrea, Somalia, and Arabia. The Eritrean variety of frankincense smells better than others and is believed to be the incense of ancient times. Eritrean incense may have been taken to Bethlehem, by the wise men when they came with gifts of "gold, frankincense, and myrrh."

Adi Quala and the South

An hour's bus ride south of Adi Ugri was another Peace Corps town called Adi Quala (spelled Adi Kwala on Google maps). Herm Nibbelink and Keith Wittenstrom were the Peace Corps teachers there, and Herm made up a song about Adi Quala.

Come a' rattling down there on the bus,
Come a' rattling down tomorrah,

JOURNEY TO ETHIOPIA: 1962-1964

We'd love to have you visit us
In the town of Adi Quala.
If you had walk-ed down the street
You would have realiz-ed
The man with shoes upon his feet
Was really ceeviliz-ed.

The song's line about a man being civilized because he had shoes was based on the fact that many men, women, and children had no shoes and went barefoot all the time. The soles of their feet were toughened into thick callouses. A student told me it was important to have tough feet so you could run barefoot over sharp stones to escape an enemy.

Sandals made from automobile tires were popular, but factory-made shoes were rare among the students. Some people wore soft sponge rubber sandals with a strap between the first two toes to hold them on.

South of Adi Quala, the road zigzags down a steep escarpment and continues into Ethiopia.

Near the southern border of Eritrea, there was a field in which stones were stacked four or five high. The stacked stones were thought to fend off evil spirits. It seemed it was working. I didn't see any evil spirits in that particular place. (The stones may have been stacked simply to make room for planting crops.)

Eritrea by the Sea

The Red Sea is warm and teeming with fish, crabs, coral, and a variety of other sea creatures. Eritrea's name is derived from the ancient name for the Red Sea. The Romans called the Red Sea "Mare Erythreum," and the Greeks called it the "Erythræan Sea." It may have been called "red" because of algae in the water that turn pink when they bloom. Another theory about the Red Sea is based on the four colors by which directions were named by ancient people. Black, red, green, and white were the colors for north, south, east, and west; and the Red Sea was to the south of that ancient culture.

The narrow-gauge railroad from Asmara down to Massawa was built by the Italians during colonial times. The fastest ride to Massawa was on a *littorina*, a passenger rail car powered by a gasoline engine. An engineer sat in a driver's seat at the front and was prepared to throw on the brakes if anything hazardous was on the tracks: cars, trucks, pedestrians, animals, or large rocks. The roaring *littorina* took passengers on a spectacular, three-hour ride through mountains; over Roman-style arched stone bridges; and across a flat, parched desert near the sea. The track traveled 73 miles through 39 tunnels, descending 7,628 feet from the cool, thin air of Asmara to the simmering heat of Massawa.

The littorina shared the tracks to Massawa with trains pulled by slow coal-fired, steam-powered engines. Towers and cables beside the tracks were left from the aerial tramway the Italians built in 1935 for their invasion of Ethiopia. The cables swooped from tower to tower across mountain valleys and the parched desert, but the tramway had been shut down years earlier.

At a rest stop at Ghinda, halfway to Massawa, a small shop at trackside sold snacks, orange Fanta soda, and cups of water and tea. People did not line up single file like you would see in the States. Instead, they stood in a fan-shaped crowd around the service window, and they then filtered to the window to be served. When the crowd subsided, I eased my way forward, but I wasn't allowed to buy a Coke until the last local person had been served.

The littorina went to Massawa, one of the hottest ports in the world. At Massawa, the average temperature throughout the year is 86°F, and daytime temperatures in summer can be nearly 120°F. Even at night, the city shimmered with heat.

Massawa's architecture and culture is like what you would find across the Red Sea in Yemen or Arabia. Shuttered balconies above the narrow city streets may have concealed watchful eyes.

The Coal Mine

Coal for the steam-powered trains in Eritrea did not have to be imported from a faraway country. On a bike ride north of Adi Ugri, Isaac took me to see the entrance of a coal mine. Men pushed empty wheelbarrows into a tunnel and came out with loads of coal. The mining inside the mine was done entirely by hand with picks and shovels.

Visits to Massawa

Massawa is one of the hottest ports in the world. The five Adi Ugri volunteers made a weekend trip to Massawa in June 1963, and it was already blazing hot. A man rowed us to Green Island at the edge of the city harbor where the clear blue water of the Red Sea was perfect for snorkeling. The water was alive with colorful fish and bright white coral. A big, flat, manta ray cruised past us near the shore, and energetic little hermit crabs with their homes on their backs skittered along the sandy beach.

The American Army had a guest house at Massawa for American soldiers, and on one weekend trip, I was the guest of a soldier there. At the swimming pool, a young soldier was rinsing a diving mask before going into the sea. He rinsed it again and said, "It still smells gasoliney." The smell of gasoline was familiar to him since he had been raised in the mechanical world of the United States. It seemed unlikely that most Eritrean villagers would recognize the smell of gasoline. If they did, they would have said it smelled like petrol.

Massawa is a mainly Muslim city, but even there I found an outpost of Christianity. John Rude and I came upon a tiny hole-in-the wall Christian bookshop on a sweltering, Massawa street. I couldn't read the Arabic over the door, but another sign announced in English that the store was sponsored by the Orthodox Presbyterian Church of America. John had attended a Presbyterian College and had already heard of this conservative branch of Presbyterianism. We stopped at the door, and a serious-looking man with a deeply furrowed brow met us. John struck up a conversation and told the man that he, too, was a Presbyterian and had gone to Whitworth College in Oregon.

"I even thought of going to Yale Divinity School," John said.

The serious missionary looked thoughtfully at John for a few moments and said in a deep bass voice, "That must have been the work of the devil."

That was the beginning of my education about the brands of Presbyterianism.

While we are dealing with theology, I should mention that the Red Sea at Massawa is the same Red Sea that the Israelites crossed farther north during their exodus from Egypt. The Bible says it was the Red Sea, but some scholars have suggested that the body of water they crossed was not the deep Red Sea you find farther south. They say the children of Israel crossed a "Sea of Reeds." I wasn't able to visit the place where the Israelites are thought to have crossed, so you had better trust your Bible for a description.

On another trip down the Massawa road, I spent an evening with Clarence and Dora Duff at the town of Ghinda, about halfway down from Asmara to Massawa. The Duffs had gone as pioneer missionaries to southern Ethiopia for the Sudan Interior Mission in 1927.

When I met him in March 1963, Clarence Duff was a spry, slim, older man. He showed me around his property and showed me where local workmen were digging a well by hand. He spoke to them in Amharic that sounded fluent to me. We sat in Ghinda's warm humidity, and he told a story.

> "I was working with a group of Christians in southern Ethiopia in the 1920s. One night some kidnappers came and took away a young boy. Later that night, we could see their campfire on a mountainside directly across a valley from our camp. The kidnappers sent a ransom note the next day by a runner. They demanded a chicken in exchange for the boy! We sent one of our chickens back with the runner, and, true to their word, the kidnappers returned the boy."

It was shocking to think that a boy was considered less valuable than a chicken.

Kagnew Station: the American Military Presence

The most foreign thing in Asmara was Kagnew Station, a high-security communications and listening post operated by the American Army. The base was surrounded by a tall chain-link fence, and it seemed like something straight from the States. There was a dining hall for enlisted men and another for officers, a chapel, a clinic, a commissary store, and most other conveniences of home. Kagnew's high altitude was ideal for those listening and communicating before satellites served those purposes. We were told that Kagnew was listening to broadcasts from Radio Moscow and from places in the Middle East and Africa. It also relayed messages from Washington to the Far East in those days before communication satellites. There were whispers among the Eritreans about the "spy station" at Kagnew, and we felt that, if the Kagnew soldiers were spies, they must be good spies, the ones on our side in the Cold War.

Merhazian Haile, an Adi Ugri teacher, was sometimes aloof and suspicious. One morning in the tea room, Merhazion said to me, "Radio Moscow says the Peace Corps people are spies. What do you say, Mr. Nyle?"

"What would we spy on here?" I asked, thinking of the cattle and donkeys trudging into town, and sometimes a car or a lorry. Where would we report on such things if we *were* spies? I didn't laugh, but I thought his question was preposterous. He probably remained suspicious of us, but he was always polite. I *think* he was wrong. At least *I* wasn't a spy.

The Kagnew soldiers and the Peace Corps teachers were young and far from home, and we had our American culture in common. I remember only men among them. If there were any female soldiers, I never met them.

At Kagnew, a soldier who had recently arrived was called "new guy" until the others learned his name. To be friendly, they might just call to him, "Hey, new guy!" It worked.

Young translators, homesick for the States, fondly remembered their training at the Monterey Language School near San Francisco. When the Kagnew radio station played "I Left my Heart in San Francisco," some young soldiers cried.

When a Kagnew man was nearing the end of his tour of duty, he was said to be "getting short," and "getting short" was exciting. We Peace Corps people could imagine the excitement of Kagnew men when they were packing for the trip home. Our day would come.

One day I received a letter in Adi Ugri from "J. W. Boggs." The letter came from an Army Post Office (APO) box number of the kind the U.S. Army used overseas. The letter began, "You don't know me, but . . ." The letter was from someone named John William Boggs, but he went by "Bill." He explained in his letter that our mothers had met at a church conference in Ohio, and they realized we were not far from each other in Ethiopia. Bill and I met a week later at a coffee shop in Asmara and had cappuccino and pastries. Bill and I became good friends, traveled together, wrote letters to each other, and later shared an apartment back in Anderson, Indiana. A line from the movie "Casablanca," described our meeting: "It was the beginning of a beautiful friendship."

Bill invited me to his barracks once or twice. In one building, there was a small table between the bunks, and on the table was an open Bible. It belonged to a soldier who was a close student of the Scriptures.

Kagnew soldiers put on a Christmas program in their gym in 1963, complete with live sheep, goats, donkeys, and three camels ridden by wise men.

The Kagnew chapel was the site of a Peace Corps wedding when PCV John Tramonti married Betty Dvorman, another PCV. Betty was forty and John was forty-two, and they seemed very old to my naïve young mind—too old for marriage. Betty was a widow, and John had never been married.

I went to the Kagnew chapel on Sunday, November 24, 1963, to grieve with many others two days after President John Kennedy was shot.

My American patriotism was stirred one evening when I was at Kagnew at sundown and saw the flag-lowering ceremony. Four soldiers marched down the middle of the street to the flag pole. Two had rifles on their shoulders. Following a strict pattern, they saluted the flag, lowered it, and carefully folded it into the triangle prescribed by military tradition. One soldier carried the flag in front of him, and the four marched away to store it until the next morning's flag-raising ceremony. We Peace Corps people didn't have traditions like that. We didn't even have American flags, but we loved our country just the same.

One older Kagnew soldier had imported a Cadillac convertible and sometimes drove it into Asmara just for fun. Another Kagnew soldier organized a work project to help villagers build a dam on a small stream near Adi Ugri. It stored water from occasional cloudbursts during the rainy season.

At the other end of the moral and spiritual spectrum, there were a couple of slot machines in the Kagnew dining hall, and I sometimes put in a few dimes or quarters to see what I would win. I was wary of gambling, sensing that I might have a weakness for it and might get hooked on it. I would put in three or four coins, and if I lost them all, I would quit. If I started winning, I would stop when I was ahead, even though my friends urged me to keep going and get rich. I avoided becoming a gambling addict and I didn't get rich.

Wikipedia explains that "Kagnew" was the name of Ras Makonnen's warhorse. Ras Makonnen was one of Emperor Menelik II's generals during the First Italian-Ethiopian War in 1896 and he was Haile Selassie's father. The word "Kagnew" means "bring into harmony" and "order out of chaos," according to the Military Insignia Products website.

CHAPTER 9

ADI GABA WITH THE MISSIONARIES

I HAD MET LUTHERAN MISSIONARIES when I attended the Swedish Lutheran church in Adi Ugri with the other Peace Corps teachers. The pastor preached in Tigrinya and then translated his sermons into English for us.

One weekend the pastor invited the Peace Corps teachers to go with him to the village of Adi Gaba, some distance west of Adi Ugri. I was the only one who took him up on his invitation. The pastor drove us west to a village called Areza, and we hiked two hours to Adi Gaba.

The crowning jewel of Adi Gaba was a beautiful little church made of blocks of sandstone that the local men had hewn from the nearby mountainside. The sanctuary's floor was shaped like a cross and was paved with smooth stones.

JOURNEY TO ETHIOPIA: 1962-1964

We reached Adi Gaba in mid-afternoon, put our sleeping bags in the church, and sat down in a nearby home for tea and roasted corn. The missionaries spoke Tigrinya with our hosts while the local women prepared dinner. The sun was lowering, and it was dark when *injera* and a meat sauce were placed on the floor in front of us. Men ate in one part of a home and the women were in another.

The food was different from any I had known. The meat sauce was reeking of an odor I never associated with food. It smelled like animal manure. I asked the Lutheran ministers, and they explained that the sauce was made from tripe, the lower intestines of a goat or sheep. I ate only *injera* and bread and tea that night, no tripe. The Lutheran ministers were experienced enough to eat the tripe.

The ministers and I bedded down on the stone floor of the church. We slept well in the Lord's sheltering arms:

> *I care not today what the morrow may bring,*
> *If shadow or sunshine or rain,*
> *The Lord I know ruleth o'er everything,*
> *And all of my worries are vain.*

Living by faith in Jesus above,
Trusting, confiding in His great love.
From all harm safe in His sheltering arm,
I'm living by faith and feel no alarm.

"Living by Faith," Authors: James Wells (1918); R. E. Winsett (1918)

It was early Sunday evening when we drove back to Adi Ugri. We could see the town's lights high on a hill, and it seemed like a New Jerusalem, the proverbial "city set high on a hill that couldn't be hidden."

A Stone Bell

On a hike southeast of Adi Ugri, we saw a stone bell high on a ridge near an Orthodox church. The bell was made of slabs of blue-gray volcanic rock about four feet long suspended by heavy steel wires from a log that was held up by upright posts. When a villager struck the stone with a

The Stone Bells

wooden club, the bell made a low-pitched, deep throated sound, the lowest note I ever heard from a bell. The sound must have carried a long way to call people to the church.

At the same sacred place, I saw a man and a woman yelling at each other across a field in a furious argument. The woman scolded the man, probably her husband, and he yelled back. This was Tigrinya at its worst—a harsh-sounding barrage of angry words.

Areza

Jackie Woodson (one of PC "girls") and I rode our bikes west one Saturday to a village called Areza. It was about three and a half miles from Adi Ugri on a good gravel road. When we came back, I told Lete we had gone to Areza. She was alarmed. She wagged her finger at me and glared out the corner of her eye.

"Arreza!" she shouted. *"Shiftas!"*

I didn't understand her alarm, but there are two villages with very similar names. One is *Arreza* with two "rr's" and the other is *Areza* with one "r." They sounded the same to me, but the one spelled *Arreza* is about thirty miles west of Adi Ugri—clearly not a place we would have gone on a leisurely bike ride. Lete probably had heard of *shiftas* or maybe anti-government fighters at Arreza and believed we had been in danger there.

"Shifta" usually means "bandit," but it could also refer to revolutionary fighters who wanted to separate Eritrea from Ethiopia.

The village of Areza looked like an adobe settlement in the western United States. It was at the top of a sandstone cliff, and a small creek flowed in the valley just below. Little kids in Areza could see that we were Americans, and they ran around us yelling, "Hello, Johnny!" They evidently had heard of American soldiers and thought we were soldiers. To them all American soldiers were named "Johnny." If we had been in Arreza, with two "rr's" the kids wouldn't have been that friendly.

Kanafana

Lul Ghebrejohannes was an Adi Ugri student from the village of Kanafana, several miles east of Adi Ugri. ("Lul" means "prince," and "Ghebrejohannes" means "the servant of John." Lul was a handsome boy who actually looked like a prince.)

Lul pleaded with PCV Jackie Woodson and me to go with him to his village. He assured us it was not very far, and we could simply ride our bikes there. We borrowed a bike for him, and the three of us set out for Kanafana on a Saturday morning. East of Adi Ugri, we rode carefully down the steep escarpment into pastureland and onto a level, sandy road strewn with sharp stones. The day was still young when a sharp stone cut a tire on one of the bikes. Lul, Jackie, and I decided to leave all the bikes by the road and hike together the rest of the way to Kanafana.

Lul assured us that his village was very near. "It's just there!" he kept saying, pointing to the next hill.

We kept hiking to that elusive hill that was "just there," and we drank some of our water, thinking we might actually be "just there." We passed hill after hill, and we asked Lul again about his village.

"It's just there," he kept saying, pointing ahead. We drank the last of our water and kept hiking. Our mouths were dry when the village finally came into view above us, up on a small plateau. Lul took us to a house where a thoughtful-looking Muslim greeted Lul and invited us in. Soon we were served boiling tea and a plate of papaya drenched in fresh lemon juice and sprinkled with sugar. Few things have ever tasted so good.

Revived by the man's hospitality, Lul led us to his aged grandfather's house. Lul must have somehow told the his grandfather that we were coming, because we were served dinner, and we were shown a room with two simple beds for Jackie Woodson and me. Lul bedded down on the floor, next to us and we all slept well.

We caught a ride back to Adi Ugri on a truck the next morning and found our bikes where we had left them. We loaded the bikes aboard the truck and were soon in Adi Ugri. The town now seemed more like a city than a village.

Senafe

I visited Senafe only once and rode through it on the bus on my final trip to Addis Ababa before leaving Ethiopia in 1964. The town is historic for reasons I'll explain, and I took one of my more memorable pictures on a hill above the town.

Sana'a is in Yemen, at the southern end of the Arabian Peninsula. Senafe sits at a high elevation on the east side of the Eritrean mountains, directly west across the Red Sea from Sana'a, Yemen. One tradition holds that the name *Senafe* is derived from a question in Arabic: *"Sana'a fee?"* ("Do you see Sana'a?") It's unlikely a person could see Sana'a from Senafe, since Sana'a, Yemen, is more than 200 miles east of Senafe. The tradition may have arisen from the hearts and imaginations of Arabs who had come from Yemen and remembered Sana'a fondly.

In 1868, the British ambassador and a number of Europeans were captured by the mad emperor of Ethiopia, Tewodros II. He had sent a letter to Queen Elizabeth I proposing marriage and was infuriated when she didn't reply. He took the ambassador and other Europeans hostage, and when word of the hostage-taking reached the British, they ordered General Robert Napier to come from India with a fleet of warships. The British built a harbor on the Gulf of Zula and built a railroad to haul men and munitions into the mountains for war with Tewodros. Elephants were brought from India to carry cannons inland to Magdala, the mountain fortress where Tewodros II had retreated with his army and his captives.

The British attacked, and Tewodros II committed suicide when he saw he was losing the battle. His captives were freed, and the British gave weapons to their Ethiopian allies. They left for India, taking their railroad and harbor wharves with them. A cemetery high in the mountains above Senafe holds the remains of British soldiers who died in the rescue operation.

The Blue Nile (1962) by Alan Moorhead tells this story. Moorhead's *The White Nile* (1960) tells of the search for the source of the White Nile.

Picture of the British Grave above Senafe

Debre Bizen Monastery

Bizen Monastery is about forty miles down the rail line from Asmara to Massawa. It is a collection of stone buildings that sit on a mountain ridge. Often shrouded in clouds, the monastery is 8,000 feet above sea level. Sunlight there is direct, so the days are warm, but nights are cold.

My friend Bill Boggs and three other soldiers from Kagnew rode the *littorina* from Asmara to the valley below Bizen. The trail up to the monastery was well-maintained and zigzagged steeply up the mountain. We were slim, muscular young men, but we were not athletes, so the hike took real effort. We paused for pictures and rested a few times and arrived at Bizen in mid-afternoon.

Monks greeted us and showed us a room where we could leave our sleeping bags, food, and water. The room was like a stone prison cell, but it would serve for the night.

We had brought canteens of water, but we found a cistern of rainwater, and thought of treating some of that water with chemicals to add to our supply. I don't remember if we drank any of the cistern water before we saw the body of a dead opossum lying in the water at the bottom. If we did drink the contaminated water, our continued good health was evidence of Divine intervention.

One part of the Bizen Monastery

Bill Boggs and Yemane Russom, my friend and houseboy, later went to the mesa-top Debre Damo monastery in northern Ethiopia. Like Bizen, it is a "men only" place, and the only way to enter Debre Damo is to be lifted up by ropes on one side of the mesa.

The Trip to "Long Back"

Of all our village visits, the trip to a wedding at the village of "Long Back" was the most memorable. It was like a trip into Bible times.

Tzeggai Woldat, an eighth grade boy, invited the five Peace Corps teachers to his village for his sister's wedding. He said she was "nine or eight years old," and he hoped we would come. He promised to make all the arrangements.

Newih Zeban

We couldn't have imagined what lay ahead. We didn't know we would travel so far in miles or hours on the way to his village, Newih Zeban, and we didn't know that we would travel into Bible times. He said Newih Zeban means "long back" in English, which may have referred to a person with a long back, or it could have meant it would be a long way back from his village. It was indeed a long way out and a long way back.

On Saturday morning, Jackie Woodson was sick and had to stay at home on the school compound. Cynthia Tse, Gloria Somple, Bill Kerske, and I boarded a bus in town with our sleeping bags and a few essentials and rode east from town to the top of a cliff. Tzeggai had sent two men to meet us with four mules for the rough trip to his village. Our guides would walk and lead the mules. We weren't experienced riders, but the mules were gentle, and we only had to hang onto our saddles to stay aboard. Our guides took us over the brink of the cliff and down a rock-covered path just wide enough for the mules. The mules picked their way carefully down to the safety of a level, sandy path at the bottom.

We had ridden the mules about two hours when several men met us and joined our guide. They led us into a small valley and up again to a plateau where there were several stone houses with roofs of logs and soil. We were in Newih Zeban.

Village men helped us down from our mules and led us into a shelter made of poles and tree branches. Colorful carpets had been arranged on the floor for seating, and tea and bread were brought to us.

The tea and bread revived us enough to see the engagement ceremony. We learned that the wedding would happen sometime later, maybe a few years later. The event we had been invited to was actually an engagement celebration where two families joined in a promise of future life. It would be a drama in which the young man would show his devotion to the young woman by "kidnapping" her to his home village nearby.

The small crowd of Eritrean and American witnesses were instructed to stand outside the shelter to see the drama. The future bride, a tiny little girl, wore traditional white Eritrean clothing. Her head and face were covered by a white scarf. Village women began trilling when the bridegroom rode up from the valley toward the girl and her family. The trilling was at its peak when the young man, a teenager, swooped up his tiny fiancé and seated her on his horse in front of him, her little legs jutting out over the side of the saddle. The horse turned, and the young couple rode out of sight into the valley. They would go to his village and spend one night under the close watch of his parents, and she would rejoin her family for a few more years until their actual wedding.

Everyone but the Americans knew what kind of party was about to begin. We were directed inside the shelter of branches and sat on carpets at one end where everyone could see us. Jars of water appeared with soap and basins, and we washed our hands. Baskets of *injera* came with generous servings of chicken, lamb, and hard-boiled eggs. Soon everyone in the house was eating and talking. Eritrean beer, *souwa*, was brought, and we Americans had our share, trusting the low alcohol content of the souwa to kill any germs.

Eating continued, and speeches began. One of the elders of the village stood and gave a speech directed to the Americans, and Tzeggai explained that he was thanking us for coming for this joyful day. He said he knew it was a long trip for us and the whole village was grateful for our visit. He went on to talk about the young couple and the village and probably about the village's crops and livestock.

When the elder's speech ended, there was a long pause. It became clear that we were supposed to respond. I can remember only some of my little speech that was translated line-by-line into Tigrinya.

"Thank you for inviting us here for your celebration," I began. "We are happy to see your village. Thank you for sharing your good food with us."

JOURNEY TO ETHIOPIA: 1962-1964

I reminded them of the trip from Adi Ugri. "You knew the trip would be a long one for us. The road was hard and stony, but you made it soft and safe by putting mules under us. The mules became our own feet down the stony path. We can only say 'thank you' for your great hospitality!"

The men murmured and tapped the ground with their walking sticks. The women trilled their appreciation. My speech was a success!

When it was time to settle in for the night, Bill Kerske and I were shown two beds made of leather straps stretched tightly on frames of wooden poles. Our beds were just outside the entrance to a home, and an Eritrean couple had already bedded down inside with their baby and their livestock. We took off our shoes but slept in our clothes, thankful for the warm sleeping bags on such a cold night. The sky above glittered as brilliantly as any starlit night we had ever seen. *The two Peace Corps girls spent that night in the place where the engagement feast was held.*

As Bill and I drifted into sleep, a cow inside the house said something in the low, thoughtful language of cows. A little later, a sheep was aroused by a dream and said something in high-pitched sheep language. Night and sleep closed in on us, and the stars looked down.

In early morning darkness, a baby cried. Its mother spoke to it softly, and the baby slept again. It seemed to me like Christmas in Bethlehem. Then all was silent except the murmurs of the cows and sheep. It was a holy night.

When sunlight began to warm Newih Zeban, the villagers brought tea and bread and hard-boiled eggs. We packed our bags and were led to the road. An old blue delivery truck roared to a stop in front of us in the road. This was the bus that would take us back to civilization. We sat on bags of grain, and other passengers eyed us silently. A goat lying behind me tossed its head and poked me in the back with a sharp horn, a reminder that the adventure was ending.

I was exhausted and thrilled, knowing that I and my friends had experienced one of the most amazing weekends of our young lives. I lay down on the cool terrazzo floor of our house and remembered that we had been at place that could have been in the Bible.

Weddings in Adi Ugri could go on all night. A booming bass drum accompanied a dance where people shuffled in a circle to the beat of the drum. The nightly sound of the beating drum became annoying after a few months, but I would pay money to hear the drum again now. The drum played a rhythm of soft and loud sounds: boom BOOM, boom BOOM, boom BOOM.

Maria Theresa thalers were used as engagement gifts for young girls in Eritrea, and they could be purchased in local shops. Named for Maria Theresa, ruler of Austria from 1740 to 1780, the coins have a long history of use as currency in Ethiopia and other parts of the world.

Towns in the Desert Lowlands

The towns of Agordat, Barentu, and Tessenei are west of Asmara on the road that goes through Keren. Those towns are at lower altitude than Keren and are very hot. John Rude and I went to Tessenei one weekend, but my visit at Tessenei was marred by a severe case of dysentery that lasted the whole weekend. I had only a glimpse of the town before we left.

On another weekend trip I went to Agordat. The most memorable sight in Agordat is its magnificent mosque. The mosque's white dome and minaret shone in the sun and evoked the mystery Americans often feel about Islam and the Middle East.

At Agordat, John and I slept on cots on the screened-in porch of the Peace Corps teachers' house. I was sleeping soundly at 5:00 a.m. when I was awakened by a loud "click" from an amplifier a couple of blocks away. The click was followed by the hissing sound of a public address system warming up. It should have sounded ominous. Suddenly a man's voice penetrated the calm morning air, calling faithful Muslims to prayer.

JOURNEY TO ETHIOPIA: 1962-1964

Allahu Akbar! Allahu Akbar! Allahu Akbar! Allahu Akbar!
Ashhadu an la ilaha illa Allah. Ashhadu an la ilaha illa Allah.
God is Great! God is Great! God is Great! God is Great!
I bear witness that there is no god except the One God.

Since it was the early morning prayer, it encouraged worshipers with these words:

As-salatu Khayrun Minan-nawm. As-salatu Khayrun Minan-nawm.
Prayer is better than sleep. Prayer is better than sleep.

Muslims fast during daylight hours during the month of Ramadan, and some won't even swallow liquids in the daytime. On a bus in the western lowlands, I saw two rustic Muslim men spitting into tin cans to avoid swallowing their saliva by daylight during Ramadan.

At the Agordat market, I took one of the more memorable of my Ethiopia pictures. Four Beni Amir men were there in long hair and robes. Two had their arms draped over walking sticks across their shoulders, and the handles of their short, curved knives were visible on their wide belts. The handle of a three-foot, two-edged sword showed above one man's shoulder. The young men were not hostile, but they were suspicious of us foreigners. I pretended to take a picture of something behind them in order to get a picture.

Beni Amir are among the many tribes living in desert and mountain areas in Eritrea and in eastern Sudan. In Eritrea there are many other tribes with their own languages and traditions. Some of the tribes are the Tigrinya, Bilen, Danakil, Saho, Rashaida, Tigre, Kunama, and Hadendoa. I had glimpses of members of only three of those tribes.

Beni Amir are closely related to the Hadendowa warriors, the "fuzzy wuzzies," that "broke the British square" in Rudyard Kipling's 1892 poem "Fuzzy Wuzzy" written in the vernacular of a nineteenth century British soldier. Kipling admired the courage of the Beni Amir when they fought the British.

On the bus from Agordat back to Asmara in 1964, I was seated in the very front, to the right of the driver, just behind the windshield, ahead of the entry door. The war between Ethiopia and Eritrean independence fighters was under way, and our bus was stopped by Ethiopian Army soldiers at a checkpoint. The soldiers entered the bus carrying hand grenades. (I shudder to think about what they intended to do if they found troublemakers.) I carefully minded my own business and looked ahead down the road. I saw an Ethiopian soldier lying behind a rock on the ground in front of the bus, pointing a machine gun directly at me. I didn't make any moves. The soldiers on the bus didn't find what they were looking for, so they let us pass. That was one of the times I didn't die but could have.

On the same trip, we saw an enormous baobab tree. The tree was round, but not very tall. The baobab stores water in the rainy season for the dry hot weather later and it can be tapped for liquid to drink.

On the same trip, at the tiny lowland village of Barentu, I persuaded a group of kids to gather around me for a photo in front of a local house made of saplings and clay. I used the picture for my Christmas greeting in 1963, implying that my life in the Peace Corps was far more primitive than it really was. (The picture fit many people's mental image of Peace Corps housing and probably increased my fame among family and friends.)

CHAPTER 10

HISTORY LESSONS

The Cuban Missile Crisis as Seen from Eritrea

THE FIVE PEACE CORPS TEACHERS in Adi Ugri had barely started teaching when one of the most dangerous episodes of the Cold War began. It was a confrontation between the United States and the Soviet Union known as the Cuban Missile Crisis. It's the closest those two superpowers came to nuclear war, and we PCVs faced it fearfully from Eritrea.

The crisis began when pictures taken by American spy planes showed there were medium-range Soviet missiles in Cuba. The missiles were believed to be armed with nuclear warheads, and they would have been able to hit cities throughout the United States.

On October 22, 1962, President Kennedy spoke to the nation about the seriousness of the situation. He said any nuclear attack on any Western Hemisphere nation would be seen as an attack by the Soviet Union on the United States, and it would lead to a counterattack on the Soviet Union. Kennedy announced that all ships bound for Cuba would be stopped and searched and would be turned back if they were carrying weapons. A blockade was set up by American warships in the Atlantic, and soon a Russian ship approached the blockade.

News of this confrontation reached us in Adi Ugri, probably through teachers who were listening to broadcasts from the Voice of America or Radio Moscow. We wondered if we should go into Asmara because of the possibility of war. There was a public phone in the tiny control room of a petrol station in the center of Adi Ugri, and I went to the station by flashlight after dark to make a call. I stumbled over a man who was sleeping on the floor of the control room. He mumbled and moved enough for me to pick up the phone. The operator spoke English and placed a collect call to the American Consulate in Asmara. The person who answered told me we should stay in Adi Ugri: there was no point in coming to Asmara, even if nuclear war were to break out.

In the face of the American blockade, Soviet ships bound for Cuba turned around and traveled northeast toward their ports on the Baltic Sea. Aerial reconnaissance showed that the Soviets were dismantling their missiles in Cuba and loading them onto their ships. By November 20, 1962, the blockade and the crisis were over, but there were still smaller nuclear tactical weapons in Cuba. To prevent the Cubans from seizing and using those nuclear rockets, the Soviets removed them on November 22, 1962.

Most of the facts about the confrontations at sea in this chapter have been gleaned from online sources including Wikipedia.

Eritrea's Union with Ethiopia, November 14, 1962

Teaching at the St. George Middle School fell into a pleasant daily rhythm. Bill and I rode our bicycles to school each morning amid herds of sheep, goats, and cattle while the students trouped out of town to the school on the footpath beside the road. Mornings were crisp and bright, and afternoons were pleasantly warm. But one day we arrived at school and found students walking around the schoolyard crying. Some pulled at their hair or tore their clothing; others stomped their feet and cried.

"What's wrong?" we asked.

"We are in Ethiopia now!" one student explained.

We're in Ethiopia now? I wondered. I thought we *were* in Ethiopia. I had joined the Peace Corps to come to Ethiopia.

The full story of Ethiopia's forced unification with Eritrea began to emerge that morning. The Eritrean parliament had voted unanimously for Eritrea to become a province of Ethiopia rather than continuing as a semi-independent country in a close relationship with Ethiopia. Rumors claimed that the members of the legislature had been bribed to vote for unification, and it was claimed that Ethiopian troops had landed at the Asmara airport to enforce the change if necessary.

Grief was heightened that day when it was learned that Ghebretensae, a popular young teacher, had been arrested and was being held by the police. Officials suspected he might lead resistance to unification, but within a day or two he returned to school and peaceful school life returned.

Unification with Ethiopia wasn't accepted calmly everywhere. An armed insurrection movement already existed, mainly in the Muslim lowlands on the west, and the Ethiopian takeover gave added life to that war. For nearly thirty years, Eritrean fighters carried on the war until Eritrea became an independent country in 1993.

Could Eritrea and Ethiopia have lived peacefully in a loose federation much longer, maybe indefinitely? If Haile Selassie hadn't engineered the vote for unification, would war have been avoided? Can Eritrea and Ethiopia ever establish a peaceful relationship? Do the histories of the two countries make them natural enemies? One can only watch and pray for better times.

Our house in Adi Ugri was owned by a man named Fezahazion Haile, a dignified gentleman on the few occasions when I met him. He favored union and moved to Ethiopia after union to take a position in the Ethiopian government. [Fezahazion Haile's wife was heavy-set, and Lete described her as "kenday harmaz," "how much elephant" or "as large as an elephant."]

Eritrea and Ethiopia Histories

The unification that took place on November 14, 1962, is part of the larger story of this part of the world. The histories and cultures of Eritrea and Ethiopia have been intertwined since ancient times. *That history is too vast for this book, but online searches of any unfamiliar words you see here will tell you more. It is a large, interesting history.*

Eritreans and Ethiopians are sometimes called "Habesha" because their languages, Tigrinya and Amharic, both have roots in the ancient liturgical language, Ge'ez. Speakers of Tigrinya and Amharic usually can speak both languages. Though related by language and culture, relations between speakers of the two languages have sometimes led to warfare over border claims and political power.

There were medieval aspects of the Habesha culture, especially in Ethiopia. Emperors and kings have arisen and fallen, the church and government were deeply intertwined, farming still followed medieval patterns, and Christianity and Islam lived side by side, usually in peace. The liturgical language, Ge'ez, has a role in Ethiopia similar to the Latin basis for Romance languages like Spanish and Italian. Those languages originated from the Latin of the Roman Empire.

The legend of the Queen of Sheba is valued by Eritreans and Ethiopians alike. The story is told in the Kebra Negast (The Glory of the King), a 700-year-old national epic. It tells how the Queen of Sheba and King Solomon met. According to the legend, the Queen of Sheba heard of King Solomon and his glory and went to Israel to see him. A union between Solomon and Sheba produced a son who returned to Ethiopia with the biblical Ark of the Covenant. That son became King Menelik I, the legendary founder of the Ethiopian royalty. Menelik II (1844–1913) claimed direct descent from them. A many-paneled painting from the Kebra Negast was sold cheaply in the Addis Ababa markets.

CHAPTER 11

CHRISTMAS 1962

CHRISTMAS 1962 COULD HAVE BEEN a time of nostalgia and homesickness for Peace Corps volunteers, but the five Adi Ugri Peace Corps teachers celebrated. In preparation for Christmas, we shopped in Asmara and gave each other gifts.

There were no pine trees near Adi Ugri, so we cut a large sisal bush and used it for a Christmas tree. Rope and twine are made from sisal fibers, but this particular bush had a higher calling. Ribbons and other homemade decorations made our sisal tree look festive, almost like a Christmas tree. We had an American meal that day, and we all dressed up in our *libs habesha*, clothing of Eritrea.

When we decorated our sisal bush, I was so inspired that I sang "O Holy Night." My voice echoed in the girls' living room. When I finished, there was no applause, only sighs of relief when my singing ended.

On Christmas Eve, three American soldiers came, and we all climbed into their jeep for the trip into town for the late-night mass at the Catholic church. The incense and Latin chants were new to me and seemed like things from the Middle Ages. On the way back to the school, a hyena scampered across the road ahead of us.

JOURNEY TO ETHIOPIA: 1962-1964

Left to right: Nyle Kardatzke, Cynthia Tse, Goria Somple, Jackie Woodson, Bill Kerske

Back row from left to right: Nyle Kardatzke, Kagnew man, John Rude, Bill Boggs
Front row from left to right: Jody Donovan, Katie Schultz, Gloria Somple

Gondar and the Blue Nile Falls, 1963

At Spring Break in March 1963, Bill Kerske suggested we take a trip with our friend Isaac south to Gondar and the Blue Nile Falls, nearly five hundred miles to the south in Ethiopia. Isaac knew a truck driver named Yirase ("yi-rah-say" – "my king") from the man's previous trips through Adi Ugri, and he arranged for Yirase to pick us up in front of our house at nightfall. Yirase's truck was loaded with bags of cement for construction of an electricity generating plant at the Blue Nile Falls, a two day drive from Adi Ugri. We climbed up on top of the bags of cement with our sleeping bags, jackets, and very little else. The truck roared off to the south while stars shone silently above.

The truck stopped briefly in the middle of the evening, and I traded places with the driver's helper and rode in the cab with Yirase for an hour. Yirase spoke little English but he was cordial and seemed to enjoy my company as he guided the truck over potholes and around curves in the winding road. South of Adi Quala, the next town to our south, we zigzagged several hundred feet down a steep escarpment and continued on a gravel road toward Ethiopia. At the next stop I climbed back on the load with Isaac and Bill Kerske, and we prepared to sleep through the night. To avoid rolling off the truck in the night, we slipped our arms and shoulders under the ropes that held the load on, and we fell asleep.

The truck stopped in the early morning hours, and we were awakened by silence and sunshine. We pulled our arms and legs from under the ropes and sat up to see our surroundings. We were in a small village, and the smell of smoke from a tea house was welcome.

I reached into a pocket for my wallet. It was gone! I frantically poked into the gaps between the bags of cement.

"What's wrong?" Isaac asked.

"My wallet! My wallet!" I yelled.

"Water? You want water?" Isaac asked.

"No! My wallet!" I yelled.

Then I remembered I had been in the cab with Yirase, and I went there. The wallet had slipped from my pocket and was on the floor next to my seat. The crisis ended, we had breakfast of bread and tea, and the trip continued.

JOURNEY TO ETHIOPIA: 1962-1964

Later that morning we passed through a tiny village and saw a woman was breaking firewood by throwing a large rock on branches that were propped on another rock. This seemed a primitive way of cutting firewood. It seemed to call for the modernization we hoped to bring about through our teaching, far-fetched as that sounds.

Farther south the truck roared around curves in the mountains of Begemder as we neared the city of Gondar. Black baboons gazed at us from a hillside, and we returned the favor. Farther south, we passed a spectacular group of tall vertical rocks that had been the cores of ancient volcanoes thousands of years earlier.

Our truck stopped beside a small roadside shop, and we bought bottles of warm Coca-Cola. That may have been the day when I coined the phrase, "Coca-Cola is the fluid on which American imperialism floats." (I don't think anyone has quoted me.)

In a patch of open country, the truck stopped beside a rustic-looking Ethiopian man. Isaac shouted to him in Amharic, "What country is this?" which is like asking what state or region it is. The man shouted, "'Topia!" Isaac snapped his fingers and laughed. We all laughed. At least he knew he was in Ethiopia.

About noon we stopped at a house in open country, and our driver went to the door and asked for lunch. We were invited in, and a very black Nilotic woman prepared the food. She was obviously from another part of the country, maybe even from Sudan. Isaac asked a few questions and then leaned over to me and said, "This woman is a slave."

Haile Selassie had outlawed slavery in 1935, but enforcement had been spotty. The woman probably could have left that family, but her needs must have been met at that home without a cash salary.

Isaac found rooms for us at a cheap local hotel in Gondar, and we went out for dinner. In the restaurant, I saw a Peace Corps man I recognized from our training time at Georgetown University, but I didn't know his name. Isaac and I took a table, and I watched for the man to leave. He passed near our table and glanced my way. I waved to him and said, "Hi." He said "Hi" and continued out of the restaurant. Isaac was scandalized.

"Pow, pow, pow! He didn't even shake you!" Isaac whispered.

"No," I said, but I didn't care. We Americans are used to casual greetings, but that would never do for Ethiopians. Their greetings can go on for several minutes with repeated greetings, hugs, handshakes, and questions about one's health, relatives, cattle, crops, the weather, and more.

From Gondar, the truck continued south along the east side of Lake Tana, the source of the Blue Nile River. Water flows nineteen miles south from the lake to the Blue Nile Falls.

Some geographers have observed a path of water moving through Lake Tana from a stream on the west side of the lake to the south end and have claimed that little stream is really the source of the Blue Nile.

The Blue Nile Falls descends 145 feet in two steps and ends in a deep canyon. Isaac, Bill Kerske, and I hiked down from the road to a large pool between the two falls. Water falling from the upper falls created a sparkling mist that gives the falls their Amharic name. The mist from the falls can look like smoke, so the falls are called the "smoke of the Abay." *Tis* is the Amharic word for smoke, and *Abay* is the Amharic name for the Blue Nile. In Amharic, the falls are the *"Tis Abay"*.

The author at the base of the upper falls

While Yirase and his helper unloaded the cement bags at the construction site, Isaac and I took a trail to the edge of the lower falls. Isaac wanted to look into the canyon below the lower falls, so I followed him on a narrow footpath that led around the pool between the upper and lower falls. Isaac took a few steps onto a narrow ledge beside the lower falls and asked me to take his picture. I went carefully around Isaac onto the narrow ledge and looked back to take his picture. The ledge where I stood was narrow, smooth, and wet, and it sloped slightly toward the river far below. Isaac struck a pose, and I took two pictures and walked carefully back to the safety of the gravel path.

Isaac on the ledge at the Blue Nile Falls

That slippery, slanted path has haunted me all these years. If I had slipped and fallen into the Blue Nile, my body would have been washed far down the river and probably would never have been found. If my body had reached calmer waters in the Sudan, it might have been dinner for hungry crocodiles.

I was young and adventurous, and the moment of danger passed. That was another time I didn't die.

Below the Falls, the Blue Nile makes a wide loop to the southeast before curving back west to the Sudan. The Blue Nile and the White Nile meet at Khartoum in Sudan and continue north to the Mediterranean Sea as the Nile River.

The White Nile flows north out of Lake Victoria in Uganda before losing itself in the Sudd, a vast swamp in South Sudan. It then flows north into Sudan's desert and joins the Blue Nile.

On our way south to the falls, we had passed through the dusty town of Bahir Dar, about 30 miles from the falls. Bahir Dar was a beehive of activity and seemed like a town from the American West: dusty, busy with people, and exciting.

We couldn't find a hotel in Bahir Dar, but a friendly tavern owner allowed us to sleep on cots in a hallway behind a counter where drinks and meals were being served. It was the best lodging we could find.

Our sleeping quarters reminded us of a bawdy song that pleads, "Remember your mothers and sisters, boys, and let her sleep under the bar." We didn't sing the song that night.

The next morning, Isaac went around the town hunting for a nephew of his who had come to Bahir Dar hoping for work. Isaac suspected the young man was running out of money and out of luck, so he wanted to take him back to Adi Ugri. He asked questions and got directions that led Isaac through the milling crowds to his nephew, a man of about thirty. They exchanged customary greetings, and we all boarded the bus. We took seats toward the front, and we were on our way.

When we reached Gondar, Isaac sent his nephew on to Adi Ugri on the bus while he, Bill, and I spent another night in Gondar. We wanted to see the 17th Century Portuguese fortress. (You can see it online.)

On a street next to the fort, we met a man wrapped in tattered clothes and a colorful scarf. "This man is a monk," Isaac told us, and he struck up a conversation with the man. The man spoke Amharic, and Isaac laughed and snapped his fingers as the man's stories rolled on and on. The monk then began to sing.

"Haile Selassie, eee-eee!" he sang, repeating the emperor's name several times in the song.

"What was he saying?" I asked. "What was the song about?"

"Pow, pow, pow!" Isaac said. "He was just praising our emperor," Isaac explained.

He thought a moment and added, "But in a good way!"

Leave it to Isaac to appreciate the emperor's role as a ruling king with great power that Isaac might have otherwise resented, but he saw value in the emperor's stabilizing and modernizing reign. If Isaac were living today, he might find the emperor's value even greater now.

Somewhere in the Ethiopian highlands, we saw a tractor pulling a plow in a large, level field at a government experimental farm. It seemed out of place. All the other plows I had seen in Ethiopia or Eritrea were hand-guided plows pulled by oxen.

Our bus roared north over the same roads that had taken us south, and the trip ended back in Adi Ugri. School soon resumed, and we awaited the rains of June 1963.

The trip had been "wonderful," something unusually good, the only meaning we Americans know. That word "wonderful" didn't always have a happy meaning for Eritreans. They took it to mean "full of wonder," or "it makes you wonder." When Isaac heard of a tragic or outrageous event, he might say, "Wonderful!" He didn't mean it was a good thing. He meant it made you wonder because it was so shocking and unusual.

Barf Bags to Gondar

In March 1964, the Peace Corps sponsored a debriefing conference in Gondar for Peace Corps teachers who would soon leave the country. I had stayed in Adi Ugri for two years, and I was sent to the weekend conference.

The conference itself wasn't exciting. There may have been a written questionnaire about the best and worst aspects of our experiences in Ethiopia, and we may have been asked for advice to give future volunteers, but I remember none of that.

The most memorable event on the Gondar trip was the flight from Asmara to Gondar. About a dozen of us from Eritrea were flying there on an old DC-3, a small two-engine plane that might have been built during World War Two. We took off from Asmara in early afternoon when the mountains below us were heating in the sun. Updrafts above the mountains lifted and dropped the plane every few minutes. An unlucky

European stewardess had been assigned to the flight, and when we were airborne, she dutifully began to serve plastic cups of Coca-Cola. When she had served the passengers at the front, the plane was hit by an especially strong updraft. The plane heaved upward and then dropped like a rock. Coca-Cola flew up and hit plane's ceiling, and the liquid began to slide toward the back of the plane, dripping on passengers along the way. Some of the passengers in the middle of the plane hadn't seen the Coca-Cola hit the ceiling, and they thought the liquid falling on them was coming from airsick passengers they thought had thrown up near the back of the plane. That made them sick, and they grabbed airsickness bags (those so-called "barf bags"), buried their faces in the bags, and threw up.

I was seated near the back of the plane and the Coca-Cola didn't reach me. It was a sadly comic scene, and it was the most memorable event of the debriefing conference.

Danger and Death

The trip to Gondar and the Blue Nile Falls went well, but death on the Ethiopian roads was never far away.

Yirase, the truck driver who took us to the Blue Nile Falls, was killed when his truck left a winding mountain road and plunged into a canyon. He may have fallen asleep at the wheel, or his brakes might have failed, or he might have simply misjudged a turn on the winding road.

Debesai was a genial, handsome man who ran the pharmacy near our house in Adi Ugri. Debesai and the man who ran the billiardi bar in Adi Ugri were killed on the road to Asmara when their car veered off the winding Asmara road and tumbled into a deep valley.

On a sunny Sunday afternoon, the bus from Asmara to Adi Ugri suddenly slowed, then crawled forward. Traffic was stopped in one lane, and people stood on both sides of the road wailing and crying. The body of an older woman was lying in the road in a pool of blood. She had fallen from a truck and was run over by another truck that was following closely. The entire village had come out to grieve her death.

On a Saturday morning bus ride into Asmara, I was seated next to a window on the side of the bus. We were entering Asmara when the bus hit the head of a man who had been walking along the edge of the road. The driver slammed on the brakes. Passengers opened the door and dragged the unconscious man onto the floor of the bus in front of me. The bus raced off to a clinic. He probably died there.

Phil Dorrance, a friendly young Kagnew soldier, visited us a few times when he rode his motorcycle down from Asmara. He was killed when he was racing an Italian in a car down the Massawa road on his motorcycle. Phil was ahead of the Italian's car when he lost control, fell, and hit his head on one of the concrete kilometer markings. The Italian driver came upon Phil's bleeding body and reported the accident. Phil had died instantly.

In spring 1964, Ethiopia changed from driving on the left, as in England, to driving on the right-hand side of the road, as in the United States. The change was well-publicized, and buses had signs on their front bumpers in Amharic, Italian, and English for several weeks reminding people to plan to drive on the right. On the appointed day, all traffic in the empire stopped for a few minutes at 6:00 a.m. Cars, trucks, motorcycles, and donkey carts carefully crossed to the right-hand side of the road all over the country, and traffic started again. There was one minor accident in Addis Ababa, and it was the only mishap. It was a governmental triumph.

Gesatchew

At the St. George School, most classes were taught in English starting in the seventh grade, and Amharic was taught as an academic subject. One of the Amharic teachers was from a remote village somewhere southwest of Addis Ababa. Gesatchew was slim and tall with a broad forehead and close-cropped hair. He was friendly and fun to talk with.

Gesatchew's schooling had begun in his home village, and by the end of eighth grade it was clear that Gesatchew was an especially bright boy. In a competitive exam, he placed so highly that he was admitted to a boarding high school in Addis Ababa, a long distance from his village. His father took him by mule to a road where he boarded a bus for Addis Ababa. He would stay at the school until the Christmas break three months later.

In Addis Ababa, Gesatchew began to learn the ways of the city and the wider world. He learned to wear Western slacks, shirts, and shoes instead of typical Ethiopian clothes of white cotton, knee-length pants, and a robe around his shoulders. He told me that if he had worn Western clothing to his village, the villagers would have thought he was naked. It wouldn't have seemed to be clothing to them.

Back in his home village, people wondered what Gesatchew was doing in Addis Ababa, the city where the king lived. They thought he talked with the king often. He might even have tea with the king. They knew little of city life, but they had seen airplanes fly over their village. The planes were so high that they looked small, like birds, so the villagers called them *neferite*, meaning "little flyer," but they knew the planes were large enough for people to ride in them. People thought Gestachew would fly over the village someday.

Every time an airplane flew over Gesatchew's village, the people thought it must be him passing by. Why else would a plane fly right over *their* village? Maybe Gesatchew has his own airplane, they thought.

"Gesatchew is passing!" they'd shout, and they felt proud to know he was so successful in the big world.

One day an airplane flew over, and someone threw an empty cigarette package from the plane. Village children found the package and brought it to the village leaders. They kept the cigarette package until the end of the school term when Gesatchew would return. Gesatchew was the only person they knew who could write, so they knew the cigarette package must be a letter from him. When he came at Christmas, they brought out the cigarette package yelling, "Gesatchew! We got your letter!"

Gesatchew was puzzled and asked to see the letter. He must have laughed when he saw the cigarette package, and he enjoyed telling the story.

The cigarette package story was ironic, because Gestachew didn't smoke and was rigidly opposed to smoking. Gesatchew did not approve when some of the teachers smoked cigarettes in the teacher's lounge at school, and he didn't want to encourage smoking in others. He explained his opposition to smoking to me, saying "Mr. Nyle, if a man asks me to hand his packet of cigarettes to him across the table, I take out my pen and slide the packet to him. Mr. Nyle, I won't even *touch* cigarettes!"

Smoking has become rare in the United States in recent years, and maybe it's rare now in Eritrea. When I visited Eritrea in 1994, no one was smoking in public places. In the early 60s, there was a brand of cigarettes in Ethiopia called "Ten Cent

Cigarettes." They were very thin and came twenty to a pack. They sold for ten Ethiopian cents per pack, the same as four cents American. You could get cancer cheaply on Ten Cent Cigarettes.

Ethiopian cigars were hand-rolled and dark brown. They sometimes smelled like burning hair because men who made them sat and rolled the cigars on their thighs, and leg hair was sometimes rolled in with the tobacco.

A Ride on a "Vomit Comet"

Someone coined the term "vomit comet" for the buses we rode in Ethiopia. Local Ethiopians as well as foreigners got sick in buses on the winding mountain roads, and stories were told about motion sickness on the buses.

A visiting American spent a couple of nights at the Peace Corps transient house in Asmara and told three of us Peace Corps people about his bus trip from Addis Ababa to Asmara. The bus was full, and a very dirty older Ethiopian woman came aboard and sat on the American man's lap. The swerving, jostling bus made the woman sick, and she suddenly turned *toward* the man and vomited all over his American jeans. He lifted the woman up and made her stand. In the middle of the passengers, he took off the vomit-splattered jeans and *threw them out the window* of the speeding bus.

An astonished passenger asked, "Were those good jeans?"

The man answered emphatically, "They were!"

He pulled another pair of pants from his luggage, put them on, and sat down again. For the rest of the trip, he didn't let the woman or anyone else sit on his lap.

Blue jeans were highly prized in Ethiopia and were a foreign luxury that was hard to come by. Jeans went by the nickname of "jungalais," a term whose origin has so far evaded my online search.

CHAPTER 12

SUMMER 1963 IN THE MIDDLE EAST

Cyprus

THE QUIET DAILY DUTIES OF teaching middle school science allowed my 23-year-old mind to wander outside the classroom. I had visited a few nearby cities and villages, but I wanted to see parts of the larger world outside Ethiopia. I began to plan a trip to the Middle East in spring 1963. I knew the two years in Ethiopia would pass quickly, and I wanted to travel while I was in that part of the world.

With help from an Italian travel agency in Asmara called *Ufficio Viagi* ("official voyage") the highlights of the trip took shape. It would start with a flight out of Asmara and would include Cyprus, Lebanon, Syria, Jordan, Cairo, southern Egypt, and Khartoum in the Sudan before the return to Asmara.

For three months I made a hobby of planning the Middle East trip in those days before the internet, Google, and Wikipedia. Most of my information came from the helpful Italian gentleman at the *Ufficio Viagi* travel agency.

As I made plans, I told other Peace Corps teachers, and by summer there were five of us on the trip: Bill Kerske, Toby Page, John Rude, Linda Hughes, and me. We departed the Asmara airport on an Ethiopian Airlines flight in a Boeing jet and by noon we were enjoying airline lunches high above the Sudanese and Egyptian deserts.

We had reserved rooms for one night at a downtown hotel in Cairo, and we checked in under the steady gaze of Jamal Abdel Nasser's portrait behind the desk. (In fact everywhere we went in Egypt we saw portraits of Nasser, Egypt's president.) We had time for only a little exploration before dinner and an early bedtime.

We had paid in advance for our rooms, but on Sunday morning, a man at the hotel's front desk wanted us to pay for our rooms again before we left. There was a small uproar in the lobby while Nasser's portrait looked on. We somehow escaped and were off to the Cairo airport.

We had tickets for the once-a-week Sunday afternoon flight from Cairo to Nicosia, Cyprus. Our flight was on a small, twin-engine propeller-driven plane. The most memorable fact about that flight, other than the fact that we made it alive, was that there were boxes of freight piled high at the back of the plane behind the passenger seats. The boxes were not strapped down, just stacked there, trusting the flight and landing to be smooth. A sudden stop in a crash, would have ended that trip and all other trips for us. *The flight landed safely, or I wouldn't be here to tell you about it.*

In Nicosia that night, after checking into our hotel, our excited little mob met for dinner on the vine-covered patio of a cozy little restaurant. We were so excited to be away from our duties in Ethiopia that we laughed and told stories so loudly that other customers were offended and moved to tables farther away. They mumbled insults as they moved, but what did we care? In our excitement, we couldn't calm down until well after our dinners had taken effect.

We hadn't planned the details of our three days in Cyprus, so we were free to roam. The next morning, we took a bus to Kyrenia on the north coast of the island. Kyrenia Castle sits high on a mountainside above the town. It was taken over by Crusaders on their way to the Holy Land in 1191 A.D. under the leadership of King Richard the Lionhearted of England.

The next day, a bus took us to a town called Famagusta on the eastern end of Cyprus. The ruins of ancient Salamis were nearby on the eastern coast, and John Rude was the only one who knew about Salamis from a brief Bible passage. He even had a Bible with him, and he read the relevant sentences to us from Acts 13:5. "When they arrived at Salamis, they proclaimed the word of God in the Jewish synagogues. John was with them as their helper."

After seeing Salamis, the others returned to Nicosia, but I wanted to see as much of the island as possible. I boarded a bus and traveled along the south coast and passed through the cities of Larnaca and Limassol. From Limassol the road turned north through the cool air and fragrant cedar trees of the Troodos Mountains to Nicosia.

We were in Cyprus during a peaceful time. Just two years later, in 1965, war broke out between the Muslims and the Christians, and in 1974 the island was divided with Muslims controlling the north and east and Christians in control of the south and west.

Beirut— "Paris of the Middle East" and Damascus

After four days in Cyprus, we flew to Beirut, Lebanon. It was sometimes called the Paris of the Middle East because of its international culture and its financial center. It is a tri-lingual city where Arabic, French, and English are official languages.

Beirut is a major port, visited by ocean freighters and cruise ships from around the world. I went swimming in the Mediterranean, and at sundown I bobbed in the Beirut harbor and shared the water peacefully with a huge ocean freighter. I only admired the ship, not envying it and the people onboard. I wanted to roam the Middle East.

While we were in Beirut, a group of students from my *alma mater*, Anderson College, were at a work camp in the mountains east of the city. The American students were building a youth camp along with young Lebanese students from local churches, and I put in a few hours with them. My Army friend, Bill Boggs from Kagnew Station in Asmara, visited the camp at the same time, and he was moved religiously by the experience. It was less meaningful to me. I was at the work camp mainly to meet other Americans.

There was a restaurant in Beirut called "Uncle Sam's Place," And it was like flypaper for traveling Americans. We PCVs were not immune to the appeal of its high-quality beef hamburgers, browned onions, French fries, and chocolate shakes. We may have eaten there only once, but the food made an impression on all of us. It seemed to give us strength for more travel.

We met an American girl at Uncle Sam's who went by the name of Mike Fancher. Her name came back to me just now, but that's all I remember. If you know her, let her know I mentioned her.

Another odd piece of American culture amused us in Beirut. A video jukebox in the hotel lobby played a lively song called "The Girl Can't Help It" complete with video of a young woman gyrating along a sidewalk. (*Through the good offices of Google, I have learned that Little Richard did the vocal, and Jayne Mansfield did the walk.*) I don't need to describe her swinging motion which, as the song said, the girl couldn't help.

Damascus

While our group was in Beirut, I took a one-day trip to Damascus, Syria. There must have been open borders at the time because I don't think I had a visa for entry into Syria. I made the trip in a jitney cab with several passengers, and the driver looked like a pirate. He had a big, black mustache, a Greek fisherman's cap, and a permanent frown. He had no patience with other traffic on the highway to Damascus, and he kept blowing a musical horn to tell other drivers to make way for him and his unnerved passengers. One of the passengers was a British diplomat who stayed dignified through the wild ride.

In a jitney cab there may be several passengers, all paying the same fee but riding together for convenience and economy.

Damascus was one of the oldest and most interesting cities I have ever seen. Narrow streets teemed with people in all kinds of clothing, and shops glittered with goods. Meat was roasting on little charcoal stoves on the sidewalks, and the stone pillars of the Umayyad Mosque's courtyard made it look like a desert oasis lined with palm trees.

On a side street in Damascus, I came upon a shop called Janan and Odeh's, where Middle East curios were for sale. I took pictures of the shop and promised to mail prints from Ethiopia to the owners, and they promised to send a gift in exchange. When I returned to Adi Ugri, I mailed pictures to Janan and Odeh, and they sent a brocade tablecloth to my mother in Ohio. Janan and Odeh were as good as their word.

Jerusalem, Bethlehem, and the Dead Sea

It was a short flight from Beirut to Jerusalem. We wanted to visit the Israeli side of Jerusalem, but we couldn't because of hostility between the Muslim world and Israel. Israeli stamps in our passports could have prevented us from traveling through Egypt on our way back to Ethiopia. We asked that our visas be stamped on separate pieces of paper, not in our passports, so we could go to Jerusalem. We had booked rooms in a small, one-story hotel on the Jordan side of Jerusalem on the edge of the "no-man's land" that separated the Jewish and Muslim sides of the city. Our rooms were clean and tidy, and we used restrooms and showers that were across a small patio from our sleeping quarters.

One evening, I went to the men's side of the restroom to brush my teeth and was just leaving when an elderly British man came striding in.

I said, "Good evening."

He said, "Pip-pip!" and it sounded as though he meant it.

I stored away that "Pip-pip" in my memory just so I could tell you about it now. No one ever had said "Pip-pip" to me before or since then, and I haven't managed to work "Pip-pip" into my vocabulary.

Very early the next morning, we were awakened by the sound of machine gun and cannon fire. Something had sparked shooting across the no-man's land just across the street from my hotel window. I saw a sky-blue United Nations jeep zigzag through an opening in the concrete and barbed wire barriers into no man's land.

At age 23, I must have assumed I was bullet-proof, because when the shooting stopped, I hiked to the Mount of Olives to see the sun rise on

JOURNEY TO ETHIOPIA: 1962-1964

Jerusalem. The morning was crisp and cool, and I was high on a hill above the Garden of Gethsemane when the sun threw golden light on Jerusalem's eastern walls. I took a few pictures and hiked back to the hotel for breakfast. I didn't get shot that day, and I was glad for that.

Later that morning, our group took a bus to Bethlehem to see the place where Jesus was born. At the agreed-upon place of Jesus' birth there was a small altar deep inside a very old church. The stable and manger of Bethlehem were not there, though they had appeared in the mural in my home church in Ohio when I was a boy. I was skeptical about the location I was shown, but I was glad to be in the general area where Jesus was born.

In Jerusalem, a site called the Garden Tomb was not far from our hotel. In 1963, I was able to walk right into the tomb and see the stone slab where Jesus was thought to have been laid. The British General, Charles Gordon believed this tomb fit the Bible's description of Jesus' burial site. Others have doubted this is the actual tomb. It is revered by many Christians, and a painting of it appeared in a mural on the front wall in my church in Ohio at Easter.

General Gordon was killed in 1885 while leading the defense of Khartoum during an attack by followers of the Muslim prophet, the Mahdi.

During our stay in Jerusalem, our group went down to the Dead Sea, several miles to the east. On the way to the Dead Sea, we stopped at a tree-lined segment of the Jordan River. The river wasn't the wide river I imagined in Sunday school. It was a tame, slow-moving creek smaller than the Portage River in Ohio, and the water was green with algae. Bill Kerske had brought a wine bottle to fill with this holy water. He knelt down and filled the bottle with nutritious, hazy green Jordan River water. He packed the bottle of water in his luggage, and no gift could have pleased Lete more. She drank the whole bottle of Jordan River water, but maybe not all at one time. She suffered no illness, probably because her body was accustomed to fighting off germs more dangerous than those from the river where Jesus was baptized.

The Dead Sea Scrolls had been discovered in 1946 and 1947 in caves near the ruins of a Jewish monastic settlement near the Dead Sea. I hiked to the Qumran settlement to see the caves where the scrolls were found while my friends prepared to swim in the briny waters of the Dead Sea. To reach the caves, I walked along a narrow gravel path on the side of a steep canyon. There was a small cave at the end of the trail that was just big enough for a person to crawl into. It fit descriptions I had read about discovery of the scrolls, and that was enough for me. I crept back up the trail and back down to the Dead Sea.

While I was exploring the Qumran cave, my friends had waded into the Dead Sea and had splashed water on each other. The oily water had clung to their skin and burned their eyes. They were still trying to get Dead Sea chemicals out of their eyes when I joined them. I learned from their mistake and slid my skinny body very gently into the water. At that time, I was a 165-pound bag of skin and bones, and I could lie face-up in the dense Dead Sea water and even raise my hands and feet partly above the surface. In fresh water, I would have been lucky to keep my face above the water.

Now my flabby body would float high on the surface of the Dead Sea like an aircraft carrier.

Near the Dead Sea, our driver pointed to a low, jagged mountain and said it was the Mount of Temptation, the place where Jesus fasted for forty days and was tempted by Satan. We had no reason to doubt our driver and were glad to leave before Satan tempted us.

Cairo and the Pyramids

From Jerusalem we flew back to Cairo. The plane went south over the Sinai Peninsula to avoid flying over Israel's hostile air space. The pilot pointed out Mount Sinai as we flew over, but we couldn't even see the monastery and convent on the mountain, or any stone tablets bearing the Ten Commandments.

The bus ride from the airport into Cairo was through a hot, dusty, red haze. There were boats on the Nile River just like the ones I had seen in my Bible story book as a kid, but Cairo was a roaring big city where cars and trucks mingled with donkeys and camels. In Cairo we stayed in a cheap hotel, but we visited the famous Nile Hilton. We met a man from India there who bragged that he had taken the elevator to the visitors' gallery at the top "five times," and he recommended we see it. We balked at the price of an elevator ride and didn't go up even once. The lobby was elegant and clean, unlike the noisy streets outside. Well-dressed people seemed to glide through the lobby in complete peace.

The pyramids outside Cairo had fascinated me ever since I was a young kid, so they were my main objective. There are 118 pyramids in Egypt, and the most famous is the Great Pyramid of Khufu. It was known as the Great Pyramid of Cheops (its Greek name). I wrote a term paper about the Great Pyramid for a college freshman composition class in 1957, so I was a borderline expert. I knew that gleaming marble had covered the pyramid in its earliest centuries, and I knew that the marble had been mined away for use on other monuments. I knew that grave robbers had tunneled into the Great Pyramid and had pried open the Pharaoh's marble sarcophagus.

It was a short bus trip from Cairo to the pyramids. In 1963, access to the Great Pyramid was easy, and the massive blocks at one corner made a stairway of tall steps to the top. The blocks were about three feet tall, so it wasn't an easy climb, but I was a skinny 23-year-old, and I made it to the top. There was a level space about thirty feet square where the marble capstone had been. From the top, I could look in all directions to see other pyramids and other ruins. The desert was to the west, and the irrigated Nile Valley was to the east. The view from the top was like what I had imagined years earlier in Ohio.

Down on the ground, visitors could walk to the broad eastern side of the pyramid and go inside to see the burial chamber. Electric lights lit the way up a long staircase to the Pharaoh's burial chamber. His massive granite sarcophagus was on a stone pedestal in the center of the chamber. A corner of the sarcophagus had been chipped away by the ancient grave robbers, and they had pried off its granite cover to steal the treasure inside.

I paid a man to take a picture of me sitting on his donkey at the base of the pyramid, and another man allowed me to pay him to sit on his camel. I didn't want to think of myself as a tourist, but what else could I have been, acting like that?

Back in Cairo, I went to see the great Mosque of Ibn Tulun and the Mosque of Mohammed Ali, namesake of the boxer who became the world heavyweight champion in February 1964. Both mosques expressed quiet, reverent calm.

It was a surprise to find a Jewish synagogue in Cairo. At the synagogue, an Egyptian caretaker opened a cabinet to show us large sacred scrolls inside.

Wikipedia reports that in 2024, there are still synagogues in Cairo, though only five Jews were known to be living there in 2019.

From Cairo, our group took the train south past green fields where workers tended crops that were irrigated by Nile River water. Paddlewheels moved water between fields in some places, just as may have been done in the time of Joseph. In another place, we saw water being moved by an Archimedes screw, a slanted cylinder with a corkscrew. A man cranked it by hand to lift the water through the corkscrew and over a low dirt dam into the next field.

We spent a day on the west side of the Nile at the Valley of the Kings. There was a tent near the entrance to King Tut's tomb where we bought Coca Cola. A man near the Coke stand acted sneaky when he showed us small clay figures of mummies. We were supposed to think the mummies were valuable and stolen from nearby tombs. I bought one that looked more or less like a mummy. It has brought me good luck, I'm sure. I might not have lived this long without that little guy.

The train took us south to Aswan, Egypt, where Russians were building the Aswan High Dam. Construction had begun in 1958, and the dam would not be completed until 1971. Aswan was awash in Russians, and I saw two of them up close. A huge Russian was leading his little daughter by the hand through a shopping area. A display of candy caught the girl's attention, and she said something to her dad. He replied in the one word of Russian I knew, "Nyet!" I was glad he spoke one of my languages.

The Aswan Dam created Lake Nasser, one of the largest man-made lakes in the world. It stretches south into the Sudan, where it is called Lake Nubia. The lake flooded hundreds of villages in Egypt and Sudan as the water rose, so whole villages had to be resettled. The flooding hadn't begun when our boat made its way up the river in 1963, and the boat stopped several times at villages where people waited at the riverbank to board or to greet arriving passengers.

Our Nile River boat was driven by a rear paddle like those in Mark Twain's book, *Life on the Mississippi*. Local people on the lower deck of the boat were surrounded by their colorful bags of clothes, food, and who

JOURNEY TO ETHIOPIA: 1962-1964

knows what else. I watched people scoop water from the Nile and drink it. They may have had natural immunity to bilharzia, or perhaps the disease can't survive in moving river water. We Americans drank only bottled water and Coca Cola.

Quiet waters near the Nile were home to schistosomiasis, another name for bilharzia, a disease caused by parasitic flatworms in calm tropical waters. The disease weakens people, making them less able to do normal work.

Man-and-wife reporters from the *Toledo Blade* were on the Nile River boat. We had good conversations in Ohio English, and they took pictures of me, since they had heard of Elmore, Ohio. They published a long story in the Blade's Sunday magazine supplement, making me famous back home that summer. I was too far from Ohio to cash in on my fame.

Near midnight, the boat stopped on the riverbank in front of the massive temple of Abu Simbel. It had been carved from solid rock in about 1244 BC. Electric lights shown on the four seated giants that faced the river and lights inside revealed ancient paintings.

It is sometimes assumed that the name, Abu Simbel, was the place's name in ancient times, but this is not so. The Swiss explorer Burckhardt was led to the site by a boy named Abu Simbel in 1813 CE and the site was then named after the boy. The rising waters of Lake Nasser threatened Abu Simbel, so it was cut into large pieces and reassembled on a high cliff out of the water's reach. It stands there now, gazing triumphantly over the water.

Khartoum

Back on the boat that night we climbed into our bunks and slept until the boat stopped in early morning at Wadi Halfa on the northern border of Sudan. A tall, dark stranger (I've always wanted to use that phrase) in a turban and a flowing white robe greeted us in solemn majesty. He was aloof and professional, and he looked like someone from the Bible or perhaps from the Koran. He guided us to a waiting train a few steps from the boat.

The train glided quietly away from the river into one of the most barren, harsh landscapes I had ever seen. It was almost like the surface of the moon. The land was flat and gravel-covered, and the monotony was broken only by scattered boulders. A boy with a few goats appeared beside the track, so there must have been plants for the goats, though we couldn't see any. The train went on and on, stopping only a few times for passengers where there must have been villages nearby. The land was so barren that larger rock outcroppings were interesting and drew our attention.

Across the aisle from our group were two muscular young men in Western clothes. We learned that they were professional couriers carrying money and documents to places in Sudan. They talked seriously, and one of them opened his briefcase and pulled out a large pistol. He handed it to the other man. He looked it over and handed it back. The second man opened his briefcase and pulled out a gleaming dagger with a blade about a foot long. He gave it to the other courier to inspect. They talked about the merits of pistols and knives and put the tools of their trade back into their briefcases. We unarmed Peace Corps people had seen a little of the less-than-peaceful world.

We finally reached hot and dusty Khartoum. The Blue Nile from Ethiopia and the White Nile from Uganda meet at Khartoum to form the Nile River that flows north through Egypt. In the neighboring city of Omdurman, we saw the tomb of the Mahdi, a Muslim mystical religious leader who led a revolt against the British in the 1800s. The revolt is described in Alan Moorehead's *The Blue Nile* and in Churchill's book about the Sudan, *The River War*. The following is a paraphrase of Churchill's chapter "Mahdi Uprising 1882-1885":

> Gordon reached Khartoum on the 18th of February 1884 and at first his mission, which had aroused great enthusiasm in England, promised success. To smooth the way for the retreat of the Egyptian garrisons and civilians he issued proclamations announcing that the suppression of the slave trade was abandoned, that the Mahdi was sultan of Kordofan, and that the Sudan was independent of Egypt. He enabled some thousands of refugees to make their escape to Aswan and collected troops from some of the outlying stations at Khartoum.
>
> By this time, the situation had altered for the worse and Mahdism was gaining strength among tribes in the Nile Valley. The

only hope for preserving authority at Khartoum and the peaceful withdrawal of the garrison had to come from outside Sudan. Gordon repeatedly telegraphed British authorities in Cairo asking that Zobeir Pasha be sent to him. Zobeir was a Sudanese Arab and was probably the one man who could have withstood the Mahdi. But Zobeir was a notorious slave-raider and Cairo refused Gordon's request. All hope for a peaceful Egyptian retreat was impossible.

The Mahdist movement now swept northward and on the 20th of May, Berber was captured by the dervishes and Khartoum was isolated, and Gordon devoted all his energy to the defense of the town. After months of delay the British government sent a relief expedition up the Nile under the command of Lord Wolseley. It started too late, and the Mahdi captured Khartoum and the Mahdi's forces killed Gordon.

The fall of Khartoum was followed by the withdrawal of the British expedition, Dongola being evacuated in June 1885. In the same month Kassala capitulated, but just as the Mahdi had practically completed the destruction of the Egyptian power, he died, in this same month of June 1885. He was at once succeeded by the Khaliah Abdullah, whose rule continued until 1898, when his army was completely overthrown by an Anglo-Egyptian force under Sir H. (afterwards Lord) Kitchener.

Our Middle East trip ended with a flight from Khartoum to Asmara on a propeller-driven plane that flew between billowing rainy season clouds. The pilot avoided the thunderhead clouds because there were strong updrafts inside the clouds that could tear the plane apart. A jet would have flown much higher, above the clouds, but we were not in a jet.

When the brown desert of Sudan gave way to the furrowed mountains of Eritrea, we felt we were arriving at home. The plane settled onto the tarmac at the Asmara airport, and we had an early dinner before catching a bus to Adi Ugri. It was good to be back home with memories that seemed worthy of Sindbad.

In Ethiopia, a bus is not simply a "bus" but an "autobus." It's pronounced "out-o-boos."

Linda Hughes was the Peace Corps girl who went on the Middle East trip. John Rude and I called her "the most perfect girl in the world" because she was pleasant, peaceful, and cheerful in all situations. Linda was always a model of cleanliness. She never seemed to sweat, and her clothes were always clean. Linda could have walked through mud puddles without getting dirty, as witches were said to do, but she wasn't a witch. She taught at Keren, a semi-desert town on the western side of Eritrea. I visited her in southern Ohio in late 1964. Linda Hughes Wilson died sometime after 1976.

New PCVs September 1963

At the end of the 1962-63 school year, Peace Corps teachers could choose to stay where they were or spend the second year in other places in Ethiopia. Three volunteers left Adi Ugri, and three others arrived to replace them. Gloria Somple and I stayed in Adi Ugri for two years. These were the people in Adi Ugri in the two years:

1962–63	**1963–64**
Cynthia Tse	Jody Donovan
Jackie Woodson	Katie Schultz
Bill Kerske	John Rude
Gloria Somple	Gloria Somple
Nyle Kardatzke	Nyle Kardatzke

Cynthia Tse, Jackie Woodson, and Bill Kerske left Adi Ugri for other cities in summer 1963. Jody Donovan, Katie Schultz, and John Rude joined us for the 1963–64 school year.

Jody had a science background due to her training in medical technology. She was from northern Indiana and had graduated from Marquette University in Milwaukee. Katie Schultz came to teach English.

John Rude had taught history in Tessenei in the parched lowland desert of Eritrea in our first year, and he was ready for the cooler climate of Adi Ugri. John was personable and was a memorable housemate, especially in the episode of the "iron-eating man" (a story that appears elsewhere in this book). John's father was a career officer in the U.S. military, so John had lived many places, including Germany and Japan. He had graduated from Whitworth College in Spokane, Washington, and was an evangelical Christian.

When Jody and Katie arrived in Adi Ugri from the States in 1963, they told us about the Beatles. They were a worldwide sensation and had been on the Ed Sullivan Show on American TV, but their fame had not reached us in Adi Ugri until Jody and Katie arrived. I bought a Beatles record that included "I Wanna Hold Your Hand."

CHAPTER 13

TEACHING TALES

Geometry and Other Math

I HAD NEVER TAKEN A plane geometry course in high school or college, but I taught high school geometry in Eritrea. In grade school, I had been an average student in all subjects. In arithmetic, I learned to add and subtract three-digit numbers, and probably even larger ones. I remember an arithmetic operation called "borrowing." I learned long division. Maybe that's where you "borrow." Or maybe I learned "borrowing" for subtraction. The fact is, I was no math genius.

In ninth grade in Ohio, the curriculum called for a stiff dose of algebra. My teacher was Mr. Clarence Egert, a handsome, curly-haired young man who may have been in his twenties back then. He taught us how to solve equations for x, y, and z and other "unknowns." He taught us about positive and negative numbers and explained the location of positive numbers by pointing heavenward with his middle finger. We never forgot that.

I could have taken plane geometry as a tenth grader in high school, but I had decided I wanted to be a farmer so I chose Vocational Agriculture instead of the college prep classes. I learned useful skills as a Future Farmer of America, but my math was limited. I didn't study geometry in high school.

In my sophomore year of college, I discovered I could do algebra and analytical geometry, so I became a math major. In my senior year of college, I was sent to a school in Anderson as a student teacher. I was supposed to be supervised by an experienced plane geometry teacher. I was to watch him teach for a week and then teach geometry for a few weeks to show off my skills. Thinking of teaching plane geometry was an act of foolish pride or just plain ignorance. I had never studied geometry. I sat in the class for two days and didn't understand a thing they were talking about. I was doomed.

I confessed my weakness to the director of student teaching at the college, and I was assigned to teach a freshman algebra class in Lapel, Indiana, a nearby town. Thirty-five students followed my presentations, did their homework, and learned algebra. I had escaped the jaws of geometry.

My ignorance of plane geometry followed me to Adi Ugri. In 1963, the St. George School added a high school to its middle school, starting with ninth grade. Grades would be added each year until it was a four-year high school.

The ninth grade math curriculum I was going to teach at Adi Ugri included segments of both algebra and plane geometry. I was competent in algebra, but I had never had a class in plane geometry. To teach the class, I would have to learn plane geometry along with my students. The school had only one copy of a geometry teacher's manual from the School Mathematics Study Group that used something known as "new math." I was to teach from that book and create lesson handouts for my students. I plunged into the geometry text and found it was easy to follow. It was logical, and I could follow the logic.

The expression "geometric logic" may have entered my vocabulary that year. Also, I learned that British English doesn't use the word "math." Instead, the subject is called "maths" in British English because math is short for mathematics, which seems plural.

The school had a mimeograph machine that was kept in the girls' house at the school. I hadn't needed the machine in our first year, but it was valuable in the second year. It used stencils to print in black ink onto large

11-x15-inch sheets of paper. The stencils were made of a material something like waxy cloth. I could type onto a stencil and draw geometric figures on it with a stylus or with a ballpoint pen. The school was generous with paper and ink, and I printed enough copies so each student had a copy of each lesson.

There were two hundred ninth grade students. If there were thirty geometry lessons, I used about 6,000 sheets of paper.

When I visited the school in 1994, the mimeograph machine was still there. While writing this book, I discovered a set of my mimeographed math notes from the 1963–64 school year at my home. Finding my notes was one of my greatest archeological discoveries.

There were two hundred ninth grade students in the 1963–64 school year, seated in five classrooms of forty students each. The students had taken a placement test, and those who tested highest were in class 9A, a very bright group. The testing had been effective, but there were students in 9B, 9C, 9D, and 9E who did well in geometry and in all other subjects. Several of my students went on to math-based careers in teaching, engineering, computer technology, and even in hydrology – the science of water management.

My students were sometimes frustrated by my detailed, step-by-step geometry lessons. Each lesson started with axioms, those self-evident truths that our minds recognize and accept at first glance. The theorems and proofs of geometry followed the axioms. A student raised his hand one day.

"Sir!" he exclaimed, "We do not like your axioms!"

The student's complaint seemed so absurd it made me laugh. The other students were too polite to laugh, or maybe they agreed with the student who asked. I tried to explain that the axioms were not _my_ axioms: they were supposed to be self-evident truths used for thinking.

Another incident in ninth grade geometry stands out. I was introducing a proof at the blackboard, starting with previously demonstrated facts, as usual. While I was speaking, there was a small disturbance in the class. I turned around to find that Haile Ghebremusie, one of my brightest students, was chatting with a boy next to him.

"If you already know this, Haile, would you like to present it to the class instead of me?" I asked.

He was a little surprised, but he was pleased.

"Sure, Mr. Nyle," he said. He came to the board and developed the proof as well as I could have, maybe better.

Haile Ghebremusie went to the University College in Addis Ababa when he graduated from secondary school at Adi Ugri in 1967. He died suddenly of pernicious cerebral malaria in his first or second year at the university.

Morals Class

The ninth grade students had "Morals Class" in the final period of the day on Fridays. No curriculum was set for morals class; each homeroom teacher was to create talks or activities that in some way taught good moral lessons. This class was not intended to be religious training; Orthodox, Muslim, Catholic, and Protestant religious leaders taught religion outside the school.

I must have told stories that I thought had a moral lesson, but I remember only one of my lessons. The title of the lesson was "Good Pride and Foolish Pride." I knew that the Bible condemned pride, but in my own upbringing, pride was not preached against very often; other sins had center stage. In Eritrean society, pride could lead to an exaggerated view of one's self, and it could lead to conflict between people. For that reason, I spoke about "foolish pride." It meant setting oneself up as a measure of rightness, almost as a little god. I told the students that's the kind of pride that the Bible says "goeth before a fall.".

I knew another meaning of pride and I told my students about the good meaning as well. "Good pride" can mean taking pride in one's work. It can motivate people to do better, to do their best work. Good pride can lead them to develop their mental and physical skills, and it can help them become more mature, I told the students. I think I learned something myself from my lesson on pride.

The students seemed to take what I said seriously. God knows if I did them any good.

The Iron-Eating Man

It began with printed fliers scattered around Adi Ugri. The fliers said that an Ethiopian man was able to eat iron and other hard objects. If given enough time, the fliers said, he could cut up a lorry (truck) and eat the whole thing, one bite at a time.

A student brought a poster to school on the day of the show and asked me if the Peace Corps teachers would go. The three Peace Corps women didn't want to come into town after dark to see the show but John Rude and I lived across the main plaza from the movie house, and we decided to go.

When I reached our house that evening, John wasn't at home. Lete told me he had gone to the "cinema," so I went to look for him. A few people were outside the theater, waiting for the Iron-Eating Man's show. To John, the show was a scandal and an outrage against the modernity we were promoting in our teaching. John was outside the theater, explaining to a group of students that the whole thing was unscientific. The so-called Iron-Eating Man couldn't do what he claimed, John said, and people shouldn't be fooled. Some kids were laughing and snapping their fingers as John talked; others were simply listening. I thought it best not to argue with John in front of the students, so I went home for the dinner Lete had prepared.

John soon came to the house for dinner. He talked excitedly about the outrageous show, and I laughed at how agitated he was. He ate quickly and went back to the theater. When I arrived at the theater a little later, people were buying tickets and going in. The highest priced tickets were for chairs in a raised section at the back. Middle-priced seats were on the floor in chairs. The cheapest seats had no chairs and were on the floor at the front. I paid for a medium-priced seat in the middle.

When the Iron-Eating Man stepped onto the stage, the place erupted in applause. Soon he was popping nails into his mouth like popcorn and it looked like he was swallowing them. He broke a dinner plate and swallowed a piece of it. He explained that he had a special digestive system, unlike other men's, and his stomach could handle nails and broken dishes. If allowed enough time, the man claimed, he could eat an entire lorry a little bit at a time.

The Iron Eating Man claimed that only he, with his special digestive tract, could swallow such items. He dared members of the audience to prove him wrong. That was a challenge John Rude couldn't pass up. He marched to the front of the theater, grabbed a few small nails and tacks, and gulped them down. He picked up a piece of a broken dinner plate, took a bite, and swallowed it. A little blood trickled down the corner of his mouth. The crowd went wild.

I was laughing so hard I went outside rather than offend the majesty of John's challenge to the Iron-Eating Man. I was laughing when I talked to a group of students outside, and the Iron Eating Man's assistant stomped out to check on the commotion. He beckoned to a policeman and demanded he restore order. The policeman escorted me to the police station a few meters away, and the policeman in charge heard the story. He offered to release me if I would go home and stop disturbing the show. I gladly took the offer and went home.

Soon the gate in front of the house clanked shut, and John hurried into the house.

"I need to throw up. I swallowed nails and pieces of dishes. I don't want them to go on through!"

He was right: he needed to get the nails and dishes out. We had heard that "syrup of ipecac" can cause vomiting, but we didn't have any. John thought that water might bring up the nails, so he drank some water and tried to vomit into the toilet. He could barely get the water to come up, and no nails or pieces of dishes came up. John pulled his chest of drawers away from the wall and put a bucket at one end. He slid himself on top of the chest of drawers with his head above the bucket, and he strained again to vomit. No luck.

It was now a medical emergency. We were both beginning to panic. There was a small clinic in town manned by a young Italian doctor. John and I walked to the clinic, rang the bell, and John explained what he had done and asked to be examined. Dr. Gianni may have felt like laughing, but he listened politely.

"Let's see if you have damage," the doctor said. "We can look inside."

He led us to a room where he had a fluoroscope. It was like an X-ray machine, except a fluoroscope allowed a doctor to "look through" a patient. Dr. Gianni asked John to remove his shirt and press his chest against a glass plate. The doctor and I stepped to the other side of the machine so we could see inside John. All the usual organs and bones were there, but Dr. Gianni pointed to John's stomach. We could see nails and little pieces of the dinner plate.

Shaking his head, Dr. Gianni said, "Those pieces are small. I can't get them out, but they will pass."

"What do you mean, 'they will pass?'" I asked.

"He just has to wait a day or two. They will pass with his waste."

Nothing more could be done at that time, so Dr. Gianni offered John and me a ride back to our house. We stopped in front, and John went inside. I stayed in the car to talk with the doctor. He sympathized with John's outrage about the Iron-Eating Man. He, too, thought it was a bunch of tricks.

Summing up, he said, "These people are backward. They can be tricked easily by a man like that. They need more education so they won't believe in his tricks."

I listened silently. I remembered that none of the local people had swallowed nails and dishes. Their natural caution and wisdom kept them from doing such things.

JOURNEY TO ETHIOPIA: 1962-1964

A Haircut in Adi Ugri

A local barber in Adi Ugri cut men's hair very cheaply. I had a haircut there, but only once. The low price must have attracted me there, but I mainly wanted to show that I was a real member of the town. The moment I stepped into the shop, a crowd of kids gathered outside to see the famous *Americawi* getting a haircut.

The barber was happy to have me as a customer, and he went right to work. He doused a ball of cotton with rubbing alcohol and swabbed around my ears and the back of my neck. He picked up his manual clippers and "lowered my ears" with a haircut above my ears like I would have gotten in Ohio at that time. The kids outside howled and laughed as my haircut continued. They pointed at me and explained the marvelous drama to each other, and the barber seemed to enjoy being a star in the show. When he finished with scissor trimming, he combed my hair about the way I would have. I paid him and gave him a little extra, and I was ready to face the world.

Successful and sanitary though the Adi Ugri haircut had been, it was the only one I had there. I didn't want an audience, and I wanted a more pleasant lotion than rubbing alcohol. I got my haircuts in Asmara after that.

Manual clippers are operated by the barber by squeezing the two handles together to make the cutting blade move. Manual clippers are perfectly safe; they just cut hair more slowly and less accurately than electric barber cutters.

The picture below shows one of many kinds of manual clippers available online.

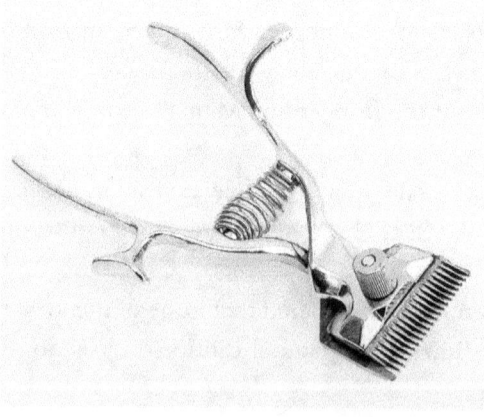

Public Health and Khasai Ghebrehiwet

Khasai Ghebrehiwet lived in a village on the east side of Adi Ugri, and he taught in one of the town's elementary schools. He was studying public health by correspondence from a college in Nairobi, and he asked me to be his tutor. He wanted me to translate parts of his lessons into simpler English so he could study them. I agreed, and we both learned about public health in the process.

One day while we were working on his correspondence course, Khasai was embarrassed to tell me, "They have asked whether we use pit toilets or indoor toilets in my country. I told them, 'In my country, most people neither use pit toilets nor indoor toilets. Most of my people just send their waste wherever they are!'"

Human waste was not the only thing that attracted flies. The droppings from cattle, sheep, goats, and chickens also helped flies survive and multiply, and flies were an ever-present nuisance. Some people sprayed their houses with a fly spray called "Flit," (pronounced "fleet") and some used fly paper and fly swatters to control the pests. Many people carried fly whisks made of a stick with sisal cords at the end. They would waive the fly whisk when pesky flies came around. A few people had fancy fly whisks with polished ebony handles and fine horse hair tied on with sliver wire, but those whisks chased the same low-class flies as the cheap whisks.

Public health people in Eritrea now spray to kill flies.

Khasai was especially fond of the song "Detroit City (I Wanna Go Home)" by Bobby Bare, 1963. He mentioned it more than once.

Yasine the "Crazy" Prophet

One day I wandered up the street in Adi Ugri and saw a crowd gathered around a man who seemed to be giving a speech. I could hear the man talking, but I couldn't understand his Tigrinya. Every minute or two, the man spoke especially fast and seemed to reach a punch line. His listeners burst out laughing, slapping each other's backs and snapping their fingers. Some nudged others and said, "B'unet!" – "He's telling the truth!"

I walked to the edge of the crowd, and someone explained.

"This man is Yasine," I was told. "He is talking about the politics of this country. Everyone knows he is mad, so the police don't arrest him. He can speak the truth because he is mad."

Yasine's listeners obviously enjoyed the show, and most of them probably agreed with what he was saying. They wouldn't have dared to talk that openly about politics themselves. After all, they weren't crazy.

In Tigrinya, "b'unet" is a word that means "by the truth." It sometimes serves the same purpose as "really?" in English conversation: "Do you really mean that?" It can also serve as a promise that one is telling the truth or is said in agreement with a truth, as in the story above.

The Long Drop Outhouse

Toileting is important to humans. Our bodies are at least 50 percent water, and we only "borrow" the solid food we eat and the water we drink. Men and women all must relieve themselves of liquid and solid waste, but customs in most cultures require that people dispose of bodily waste in private or secretly.

Some aspects of toileting were not as secret in Eritrea as people might have wished. Women sometimes squatted beside the road to urinate at bus stops on the trip to Asmara, their long dresses providing a degree of modesty. Men might urinate privately beside a bus simply by turning their backs.

Passing gas was considered especially shameful. People sometimes banged rocks together, even out in distant fields, to avoid hearing *themselves* pass gas. Passing gas in the presence of other people was unbearably shameful. A man in the lowland desert danced so enthusiastically at his daughter's wedding that he passed gas in front of the crowd. He disappeared into the desert and was never seen again.

I saw a spectacular outhouse at a village, probably one of the world's finest. If an Olympic competition were held for memorable outhouses, this one would win at least a silver medal. I'm calling it *"the"* long-drop outhouse, not "a" long drop outhouse, because I doubt there is another like it anywhere.

The geography of the area around the village was mountainous like all of central Eritrea, and the outhouse had been built on a shelf of sandstone rock that jutted out over a deep valley. The stone shelf was a few inches thick, and someone had carved a hole in it. There was no toilet to sit on, and so a person had to squat over the hole. For privacy, the toilet was enclosed by walls on three sides to form a simple outhouse. The side facing the empty valley was not walled in. Those using the outhouse had a spectacular view of the valley far below.

There was a long, empty valley below the outhouse, and the base of the sandstone cliff swept outward into the valley. Looking down from the top, you could see that droppings had been falling at the foot of the cliff for years, drying there until rain washed the droppings farther into the valley. Some droppings may have been there for years, but not for centuries.

Impressed as I was by the outhouse, I'm sure I didn't use it. One would remember such an experience for a very long time.

The Day the President Died

One Friday evening I stayed in Adi Ugri for a quiet weekend rather than making the bus trip to Asmara. My housemate, John Rude, had gone to the city, so I had the house to myself. Our maid, Lete, prepared food for my dinner, cleaned up the kitchen, and left for the evening with a frying pan of burning charcoal. Our student-houseboy, Yemane, had left for his village in the afternoon.

For my bedtime reading, I chose a *Life Magazine* article about the assassination of Czar Nicholas II and his family during the Russian Revolution. There were photos of the Czar and his family, and the article told how Communist revolutionaries had herded the family into a basement and shot them there.

As I turned off the lamp, I wondered, "What is it like to be shot and killed? How does it feel? Do you feel anything, or are you suddenly dead?"

(When I turned off my light it was 9:00 p.m. in Adi Ugri. It was 12:00 noon in Dallas, Texas.)

Saturday morning, November 23, 1963, was a typical Adi Ugri morning in the dry season. It was chilly at sunrise under a clear blue sky, and by late morning the air was warm and scented by flower blossoms and cooking fires. Lete cooked scrambled eggs and coffee for my breakfast and went to work on the laundry.

JOURNEY TO ETHIOPIA: 1962-1964

The stone wall between my house and the landlord's house was soiled brown from rain and dust, and I had bought a bucket of whitewash for the wall. I stirred up the whitewash and took it to the wall. I had splashed on only a few brush strokes when there was a knock at the front gate.

The visitor was Khasai Ghebrehiwet, my friend from the elementary school in town. I invited Khasai into the yard and began to lead him to the back yard to show off my whitewash work. As he came through the gate, Khasai glanced at my poster of John Kennedy that was hanging just inside the front door.

"There's President Kennedy," he said casually, pointing to the poster. "He's dead, you know."

I thought he was making a bad joke, but he went on.

"He was riding in a car in Dallas, Texas."

"What kind of nut would wreck the president's car?" I wondered. There must have been a fatal car wreck.

Khasai went on to say something about Kennedy being shot. He said he was "shot in the head." I knew that would be fatal. How could such a thing happen in the most powerful country in the world?

Khasai could see how shocked I was. He thought I had already heard the news.

"No!" I yelled and walked around to the back of the house, my mouth open in shock.

When Lete heard me yell and saw me staggering, she brought both arms up to the sides of her head in an Eritrean way of grieving and cried too. She must have heard about the assasination, and she must have thought I knew. Khasai slipped out into the street and went away, not knowing what to say.

I didn't know that the Peace Corps girls had gone to Asmara with John Rude, so I sat down and typed a short letter to them about the assassination. As I saw the words fill the page, I burst out sobbing. I stepped into the street and found a student who took the letter to the school to tell the girls while I quickly packed a small bag. The student returned and told me that all the Peace Corps teachers had gone to Asmara on Friday night.

On the bus to Asmara I sat in a stupor, gazing at the mountain sides. In Asmara, the clip-clop of the ghari horses seemed eerie and far away, not charming like before. I booked a room at a pensione hotel and joined some Peace Corps teachers for lunch. At the Italian restaurant, the middle-aged owner rose from his desk at the door and stood at attention as we entered. Everyone in the restaurant stopped talking until we were seated, and the place was unnaturally quiet.

That evening, several of us went to the Odeon Theater to see whatever movie was showing. The movie happened to be the 1962 version of "State Fair," set in Dallas, Texas. The movie starred Pat Boone, Bobby Darin, and Ann-Margret. In an early scene, Pat Boone is driving an open convertible, merrily singing, as they drive into Dallas:

> "Our state fair is a great state fair,
> Don't miss it, don't even be late,
> Our state fair is a great state fair,
> The finest state fair in our state!"

The movie showed Dallas as a friendly, wholesome place, and we were shocked at how inappropriate the movie was on the night after the assassination. At the pensione that night, a radio was playing dirge music from Kagnew Station Radio. The music was unspeakably sad, like the night itself.

Unknown to us that dark night, C.S. Lewis, the great English Christian writer, also had died on November 22, 1963. That news was lost in the shock and grief of the Kennedy assassination.

The probable assassin had been arrested at a theater in Dallas and was being held at a courthouse jail. The suspect was a 23-year old man named Lee Harvey Oswald who was known to be sympathetic to Communist Cuba. News of his arrest reached the world through Radio Free Europe and other international news channels, and "Lee Harvey Oswald" was suddenly a household name, especially to Americans.

The Dallas police wanted to move Oswald from the city jail to a more secure prison, and plans for his transportation had been announced by an overly talkative Dallas police official. The news had been followed by a night club owner named Jack Ruby, and he was waiting at the jail when Oswald was led out under heavy guard. Ruby admired the police and had always been a peaceable person, so they thought nothing about his being there. Suddenly, Ruby pulled out a small pistol, leapt toward Oswald, and shot him in the stomach. A photographer caught the shooting in a picture, with Oswald doubled over in pain.

I hadn't heard that Oswald had been shot when I arrived at Barbara Olsen's apartment.

When I arrived, Barbara announced, "Somebody shot Oswald!"

We sat down in front of her radio and listened as Kagnew Station radio reported on Oswald's shooting.

"Live, Oswald, live!" I yelled to the radio. The world needed to know what was behind his crime, and people needed to hear from Oswald himself. It was not to be. Oswald died and he has remained a mystery in some ways to this very day.

"How could there be two ghastly shootings on one weekend? What was happening to the world?" Americans wondered.

On Monday, November 25, we five Peace Corps teachers took the bus back to Adi Ugri while the whole world grieved. At a remote police station on a mountain ridge, the Ethiopian flag was hanging limply at half-staff.

When the bus rolled through Adi Ugri, all the shops were closed, Muslim and Christian alike. We had never seen *all* the shops closed. The Muslim shops had been open on Christian holidays, and the Christian shopkeepers returned the favor on Muslim holidays. On the day of Kennedy's funeral, everyone grieved together. Someone said later that Kennedy's assassination was the most universally grieved death the world had seen.

We five Peace Corps teachers gathered around a radio at the girls' house on the school compound that evening to listen to Kennedy's funeral on Armed Forces Radio. The funeral began at 10:30 a.m. Eastern Standard Time, or 7:30 p.m. Ethiopia time.

The next week, *Time* and *Newsweek* magazines showed Jackie Kennedy standing majestically beside little JFK, Jr., as he saluted his father's coffin. It was the little boy's third birthday. Photos showed Emperor Haile Selassie marching in the funeral procession beside the towering figure of French President Charles de Gaul.

Around the world there were many reactions to Kennedy's death. Somewhere in the Middle East a mob celebrated, but most of the world grieved.

An Eritrean man in the town of Senafe had been earning a little income for distributing dried milk to poor children for the Agency for International Development, AID. When the man heard of the assassination, he moaned, "That's the end of the milk! It's the end of the milk!"

About a week after the assassination, I went to Kagnew Station to have lunch with an Army friend. We were joined by another soldier, a man from Texas. Talk turned to the assassination.

"It was no secret that he wasn't welcome in Dallas," the Texan said.

We gulped and let it pass.

Soon after the Kennedy assassination, popular music changed from folk songs and sentimental music to acid rock and other violent music. The sixties began with the Kennedy assassination, and some would say the sixties have not ended.

Our Peace Corps group had flown from Idlewild Airport in New York City to Ethiopia in 1962. When we returned to the United States in 1964, the same airport had become John F. Kennedy International Airport. The name was changed on Christmas Eve 1963.

We were told that a black necktie should be worn as a sign of grieving. A tailor in Adi Ugri made a narrow black tie for me, and I wore it every day for a month.

CHAPTER 14

KENYA AND UGANDA TRAVEL 1964

I HAD HEARD OF AFRICA as a young boy when missionaries from Kenya visited our church in Ohio. Missionaries had taken their teaching and medical skills to Christian mission stations in Kenya, and I wanted to see those places while I was living nearby in Ethiopia.

Three other Peace Corps teachers joined me in January 1964 for the trip to Kenya and Uganda. They were Gloria Somple, Jody Donovan, and John Rude. Our flight from Asmara stopped briefly at Addis Ababa and continued to Nairobi.

I knew a few people in Kenya through my college friendships, and I had written to them before the trip. Ruben Schweiger was a college classmate of mine, and his wife Jenny was the daughter of a missionary doctor named Dr. David Livingstone, the same name as the much earlier doctor and explorer.

I also knew Gideon Wandera, a Kenyan a few years older than me who had worked with my uncle, Carl Kardatzke in Kenya in the 1950s. Carl had sponsored Gideon for study at Anderson College and Gideon had lived next door to me in a men's residence there. Gideon was in the States without his wife and children during his studies at Anderson College. After college, he returned to Kenya and held a position in the colonial government before Kenya became independent from Great Britain at the end of 1963.

Gideon offered to send his driver and his car on the trip my Peace Corps friends and I had planned to take in Kenya and Uganda. The driver knew very little English, but he was an excellent driver and guide. He drove us west from Nairobi through the Rift Valley and through tea plantations in the highlands of western Kenya.

We visited a college friend of my parents, missionary Claire Schultz. He took us on a tour of the main mission station, and we attended a church service on Sunday. The church was a large brick building, and there were about five hundred Kenyans there. The African people were well-dressed in Western clothing, and they sang beautifully in Swahili. I knew some of the songs, but the people sang them from memory.

After church, Gideon took us to a restaurant where we ate thick corn-meal balls, a food called *obasuma*. It came with chicken stew, and we made scoops from balls of warm corn meal mush. We popped the scoops of chicken broth into our mouths. The mild stew was a pleasant change from the hot, spicy zigini of Eritrea.

You can learn how to make obasuma by googling "obasuma food in Kenya."

At a clinic near the church, the name "Dr. Livingstone" appeared on an outside door. I took a picture of the historic name before we departed west for Uganda. This was not the Dr. Livingstone who was found by Henry Stanley in 1871.

The following account of their meeting is taken from Wikipedia:

> *Henry Morton Stanley had been sent to find him by the New York Herald newspaper in 1869. He found Livingstone in the town of Ujiji on the shores of <u>Lake Tanganyika</u> on 10 November 1871, apparently greeting him with the now famous words "Dr. Livingstone, I presume?" Livingstone responded, "Yes", and then, "I feel thankful that I am here to welcome you." These famous words may have been a fabrication, as Stanley later tore out the pages of this encounter in his diary. Even Livingstone's account of this encounter does not mention these words. However, the phrase appears in a New York Herald editorial dated 10 August*

1872, and the Encyclopædia Britannica and the Oxford Dictionary of National Biography both quote it without questioning its veracity. The words are famous because of their perceived humor, Livingstone being the only other white person for hundreds of miles, along with Stanley's clumsy attempt at appearing dignified in the bush of Africa by making a formal greeting one might expect to hear in the confines of an upper-class London club. However, readers of the Herald immediately saw through Stanley's pretensions. As noted by his biographer Tim Jeal, Stanley struggled his whole life with a self-perceived weakness of being from a humble background, and manufactured events to make up for this supposed deficiency. Stanley's book suggests that this greeting was truly motivated by embarrassment, because he did not dare to embrace Livingstone.

In Uganda we visited famous game preserves. We saw elephants, hippos, lions, giraffes, wart hogs, crocodiles, and several kinds of antelope. An excursion in a small river boat went among submerged hippos whose eyes and nostrils were just above the water. Crocodiles slept on the shore with their mouths wide open, as nature's air conditioning for critters of their kind.

Uganda felt dangerous in 1964, not only because of the wild animals but because of something among the people that felt violent and dangerous. I took a picture of some women in Kamala wearing colorful, flowing dresses that made them look like ships under full sail. The women saw me taking a picture and shouted angrily at me. I put my camera away and kept my distance.

The School Book Saga, 1964

My dad learned that the U.S. Navy would ship school books to schools like ours around the world. The books that my father collected were used, out-of-date, public school textbooks from schools in the small Ohio towns of Elmore, Rocky Ridge, and Genoa. My dad built six sturdy plywood boxes, filled them with books, and nailed the lids shut. He turned the boxes over to the U.S. Navy, and they shipped them across the Atlantic Ocean, through the Mediterranean Sea, down the Suez Canal, and then down the Red Sea to the Ethiopian port of Massawa. A Peace Corps pickup truck brought them to St. George School.

JOURNEY TO ETHIOPIA: 1962-1964

The school had a small library run by Mr. Asmerome, and the books quadrupled the number of books in his library.

I teased Mr. Asmerome by singing a parody of "Marian, Madam Librarian" from "The Music Man" to him: "Asmerome, Mister Librariome!" He smiled indulgently and put up with me.

Eritrean fighters took some of those Ohio textbooks into wild mountain country during the war for Eritrean independence. The fighters used the books in the schools they started in caves, tunnels, and houses.

The war had already started in outlying areas by the time our group left Ethiopia in 1964. While the war grew, St. George School was sometimes taken over by Eritrean fighters.

Shiftas

There were *shiftas* in Eritrea in the early 1960's. *Shifta* can mean "bandit" or it can mean "revolutionary," and the two meanings sometimes overlapped: a revolutionary could also be a bandit. Local people either feared or respected shiftas, depending on who the *shiftas* were.

In spring 1964 the Adi Ugri police brought the body of a large man into town and laid it in an empty lot across the street from the boys' house. The police said the man was a bandit *shifta*. The body had swollen, and it was an ugly sight.

Andarge, an Amhara school official from the Ethiopian government, was disgusted by the body and by the crowds' curiosity. He grumbled that the police should not have allowed the spectacle, but the police probably thought that the body would be a warning to other would-be *shiftas*.

Easter in Eritrea

Easter was the most important Christian holiday in Eritrea. Christmas was mainly a time when Europeans and Americans decorated their homes, sang special songs, and exchanged gifts while the Orthodox Eritrean believers stood by tolerantly.

Easter in Eritrea did not come upon its people suddenly one Sunday morning as it does for some people in the States. Eritrean, Christians practiced a rigorous, forty-day time of fasting. For forty days before Easter, Christians ate no meat, eggs, milk, butter, cheese, nor any other product taken from an animal, bird, or fish. These observant Christians ate a variety of vegetable and bean dishes during their Lenten season. No one died from this fasting, and that in itself may have been miraculous, given the low-calorie diets of so many.

The Eritrean Orthodox fast was broken at midnight on Easter morning. Worshipers came to the orthodox church carrying candles, a reminder of the Light that shone in the darkness, the Light the darkness could not comprehend and could not put out. Churches were filled, and many people stood outside churches in the chilly night. Inside, ancient chants celebrated the resurrection of Jesus the Christ and, after midnight, the feasting began.

I climbed to the roof of the men's house that night and took pictures of the procession of worshipers arriving with their candles at the Orthodox church half a mile away. The time exposure picture I took that night with a telephoto lens is my mental image of Easter in Ethiopia. Lights glowed through the church's windows, and candlelight illuminated the white Eritrean/Ethiopian robes of those at the church. The new day they

Christians at the Adi Ugri Orthodox Church, very early on Easter morning, 1964.

celebrated divided the Christian future from the ancient past. That night I saw the real Easter sunrise, like the Light of Jesus, entering the church. The picture I took that Easter night is one of the best I have taken.

Having seen the drama of the Orthodox Easter, I appreciated Easter in America more profoundly than ever before. It helped me understand that Easter, not Christmas, is the central Christian celebration. Easter became much more meaningful than my youthful perception had been, limited as it was to lilies, new clothing, Easter eggs, and special Easter music. At last, I understood the significance of the first pilgrimage to the empty tomb, newly illuminating the darkness outside. I had heard of it many times, but I hadn't really seen it until then.

The candles the people took into the church on Easter morning were made in that area of beeswax. The candles were slender, about two feet long with bumpy sides.

CHAPTER 15

STUDENT STORIES

MANY STORIES COULD BE TOLD about the lives of Adi Ugri students. I will tell you here about a few students that I knew well.

Aregai Tecle

I met Aregai on the first day of classes in 1962. He was a very good student and was in Class 8A in the 1962-63 school year, a class of students who had scored highest on a placement test. Life had not been easy for Aregai. He always wore light blue denim shorts and a denim jacket over a T-shirt, and he wore sandals made from car tires. Those may have been the only clothes he had.

When Sargent Shriver, the Peace Corps Director, visited the school in 1962, he stepped into the 8A classroom and stood directly in front of Aregai and spoke to him. Shriver asked Aregai a couple of questions and commended him for his studies, and that was an historic moment for Aregai and for the school. Aregai and others were stunned to know that he had spoken to the brother-in-law of President Kennedy.

Aregai Tecle is in the front row in the blue coat.

Most of the Adi Ugri students were very poor, and Aregai may have been one of the poorest, so he needed a way to earn some cash. I had seen dried goatskins in the Adi Ugri market and thought that maps of Ethiopia could be burned onto the goatskins. To test the idea, I bought a goatskin and asked Haile Ghebremusie to hold a large nail with pliers and heat the nail in a charcoal fire. Haile found that the hot nail burned holes in the hide as he drew, and that may have been the only goatskin map that Haile Ghebremusie made. Aregai Tecle found that he could draw a map of Ethiopia with a ballpoint pen, so he took over the map business and made enough money to keep him in school.

There wasn't much of a market for Ethiopia maps in Adi Ugri, but Aregai took bundles of them to Asmara and sold them to Kagnew soldiers, Peace Corps teachers, and other foreigners. He made dozens of goatskin maps, and some of them probably still hang in homes of Americans.

Aregai walked with a very awkward limp. He said it was caused by an infection he had when he was young. He said he had been scratched by a thorn, and the scratch became infected and damaged nerves and muscles in his legs. In 1969, Dr. Evelyn Bolin, an aunt of John Rude, heard of Aregai and his damaged legs. She helped Aregai get a visa and a plane ticket, and she found skilled surgeons to do the work. The surgery was only partially successful, but it improved Aregai's walking for the adventures that lay ahead.

At Christmas 1970, Aregai was visiting me at my wife's parents' home on the far south side of Indianapolis. While the family was preparing for a big evening meal, we realized that Aregai wasn't in the house with us. Someone said he had gone to the public school playground three blocks away with six-year old Anita, my wife's niece. My father-in-law was alarmed when he learned the two were out after dark. He feared what people might say or do when they saw a dark-skinned young man with a young white girl. It could have become a crisis, but the two returned to the house, happy about their playground trip, and the evening's joy was restored.

By 1971, Aregai was a member of my family. He was in my brother Larry's wedding on February 6, 1971, and he was in my wedding on June 12, 1971. He graduated from Anderson College (Indiana) in 1971, and he was in Elmore, Ohio, on July 4, 1976, to celebrate the Bicentennial with my parents and the whole community.

After graduating from Anderson College, Aregai returned to Ethiopia to teach high school courses and work as a curriculum expert in the Ministry of Education. He also had a part time job as a TV operator, turning on the TV and setting the sound level.

In 1978, Aregai was working for the Ministry of Education in Addis Ababa. His roommate had made plans to leave the country and had sold everything he owned for cash. Someone reported Aregai's roommate to the terrorist "neighborhood association" that was ruling that part of the city. They arrested the roommate and told him he could go free if he would tell them where he had hidden his money and give them the name of another person who was hiding money. He told them where his money was, they confiscated his money, and they shot him. He had told them that Aregai had a lot of money, too, so they arrested Aregai and told him they would shoot him if he didn't tell them where his money was hidden.

Aregai had no money, so they put him in one of their concentration camps in Addis Ababa and scheduled him for a firing squad execution.

But that concentration camp was taken over by men in charge of another concentration camp, and Aregai's execution was postponed. At Easter 1978, in a flight of fancy, the people who ran Aregai's new concentration camp decided to have an Easter amnesty. They went through the camp randomly selecting prisoners, and Aregai was one of those chosen. He was sent out onto the streets of Addis Ababa, a free man. It was rare for anyone to leave a concentration camp alive. When Aregai's friends saw him walking along a street in Addis, they nearly fainted to see a "dead man walking."

People at the Ministry of Education in Addis Ababa didn't know that Aregai had been in prison or that he had been released. Aregai went directly to the Ministry, and they found that he had received a scholarship and travel money for graduate study at the University of Arizona. The Ministry officials arranged a visa and a plane ticket for Aregai, so he picked up a suitcase and a few articles of clothing and went to see his fiancé, Negisti. They quickly got married so she could enter the U.S. later. Aregai left Ethiopia on the first flight to Frankfurt, Germany.

Ethiopia was riddled with spies and killers, and Aregai didn't feel safe, even on the plane to Germany. He looked suspiciously at other passengers, but no assassin or kidnapper showed up. At the airport in Frankfort, he hid among the shops until his flight to New York was announced. When the cabin doors closed for his flight to America, he began to feel safe in his escape.

When he arrived at the JFK Airport in New York, Aregai called me at my home in Wisconsin. I was out in the back yard with my family when he called. I recognized his voice, but I couldn't believe that it was him calling. I hadn't heard from Aregai for months, and I feared he had been killed. When I realized it really was Aregai, I fell down on the lawn and cried.

Aregai flew to Indianapolis and Mr. C. Jean Kilmer, the Admissions Director at Anderson College met him at the airport. Kilmer and his wife took Aregai to their home in Anderson and then to an apartment at Ball State University in nearby Muncie, Indiana, where he had been admitted for graduate studies.

When Aregai was settled in Muncie, Negisti flew to Indianapolis, and my brother Larry took Aregai to the airport to meet her. Aregai earned a master's degree at Ball State and was awarded a scholarship at the University of Arizona in Tucson, where he earned a Ph.D. in hydrology and watershed management. He retired many years later as a full professor at the University of Northern Arizona in Flagstaff.

One evening in March 2016, I visited Aregai Tecle and his wife Negisti at their home in Flagstaff. As we talked after dinner, Aregai began to tell about events of his life, some of which I had never heard, though I had known him since 1962. He told stories for two hours. What I have written about him here includes my knowledge of Aregai from Adi Ugri as well as things he told me that night in Flagstaff. Aregai recently retired to the warmer climate of Phoenix, Arizona.

There are many articles on the internet about "Aregai Tecle." All the entries seem to be about the Aregai Tecle I know. There can't be many Aregai Tecle's in the world.

Yemane Berhan Russom

Yemane Russom was the best of the household helpers at the boys' house in Adi Ugri. "Yemane" means "at the right hand of the king," and he lived up to his name, though John Rude and I were not kings.

When Ato Iob first brought Yemane to us, I asked Yemane, "Are you a good student?"

"Yes," he said, "one of the best."

He was right. We hired Yemane as our houseboy, and that turned out to be a good decision for us as well as him. In the 1963–64 school year, he was in Class 9A, because he had placed very high on the school's placement exam.

In the photo below Yemane Russom is at the right-hand end of the first row. There were twenty-six students in Class 9A in the 1963-64 school year. The class included Yemane Russom, Haile Ghebremusie, Aregai Tecle, Yohannes Andemichael, Tesfeledet Andemeskel, Melake Ghebra, and Tsehainesh Ghebrejohannes. Tsehainesh is in the center of the first row.

JOURNEY TO ETHIOPIA: 1962-1964

We hired Yemane for $5 Ethiopian per month, the equivalent of $2.00 U.S. at the time, plus room, board, and some new clothes. He and Lete worked together, but Lete wanted to be Yemane's boss. She even wanted him to go home with her and sleep on the floor in her little apartment near the Ethiopian Orthodox church. We knew that if he slept at her house, he would have to study outside in the cold under street lights, so we invited him to sleep at our house and study in our kitchen. He lived with John Rude and me for a year, spending his nights in a sleeping bag in our entry hall. The next year, the Peace Corps men who lived in the house gave Yemane an actual bed.

Yemane was able to stay on Lete's good side most of the time. She was once so angry with him that she wanted us to fire him. We told her we would fire her instead, and she calmed down.

During his year as a our houseboy, I encouraged Yemane to sell popcorn at the Adi Ugri movie theater to earn extra money. John and I bought popcorn in Asmara, and Yemane popped it at our house on the kerosene stove in our kitchen. He put the popcorn in rough paper cones and tried to sell it at the Adi Ugri cinema. Popcorn was not known to Adi Ugri audiences, and Yemane couldn't sell enough to keep the business going, so he shut it down.

Yemane was born in 1951, but he didn't know his exact birth date. He knew that he had been born near the end of February. When he applied for his first passport, he told the official at the American Consulate in Asmara that his birthday was February 31. That got a good laugh, so he chose February 28, 1951, as his birthdate. That worked. I have that date on my Google calendar, so it has to be right.

John and I visited Yemane's village in 1964. We met his beautiful grandparents.

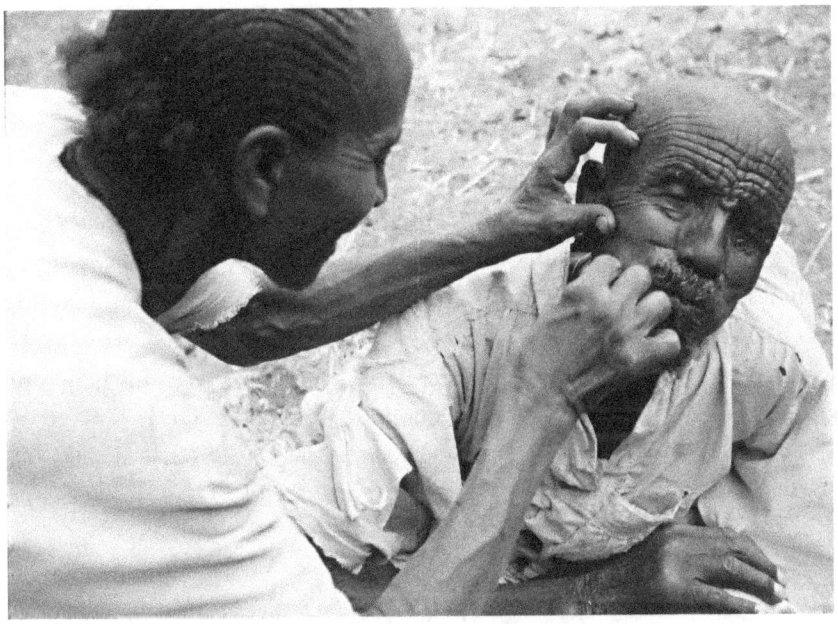

Yemane's grandmother shaving his grandfather's face

After John Rude and I left Ethiopia in 1964, Yemane worked for the new male teachers who took our places. That was his sophomore year in high school. In his junior year, he was selected to spend a year in the U.S. on an American Field Service scholarship. He lived with a farm family near Merrill, Wisconsin, and he had a dose of very cold winter weather. He came to Chicago in winter 1967 to see me with my future wife, Darlene. He returned to St. George School and graduated in 1967.

Four years later, Yemane graduated from the University College in Addis Ababa. He was hired by an oil company in Calgary, Canada, to work with them on oil exploration. That job led to his move to Houston, Texas, and he is still living there with his wife Zewdi and their daughter Selam.

Yemane's most famous project is a software program he created that allows Tigrinya speakers to write in the Tigrinya (or Geez or Amharic) alphabet on a personal computer. Those languages are written in syllables, and that's not a problem when writing in ink on paper. Writing those languages on a typewriter or a computer uses two key strokes for each syllable, one stroke enters the consonant base, and the second stroke enters the vowel sound for that syllable. Yemane's company, Geezsoft, is known and used by Tigrinya writers in all parts of the world.

Other people have sold pirated copies of Geezsoft in recent years and have made the software less profitable for Yemane.

Yemane also collects chants of the Orthodox Church. At his website, *geezesoft.com*, the Orthodox liturgy appears in English and in Geez, and it includes a phonetic transliteration of Geez. If you follow the transliteration, you can begin to learn the Geez or Tigrinya alphabet. Yemane carries on his work from his apartment in Houston, Texas. Only a few of his neighbors know they have such a hero living among them.

The following story about Yemane was written by Harold Freeman, one of the Peace Corps men who lived in Adi Ugri from 1964 to 1966. Harold was a journalist before his Peace Corps days.

Generosity

By Harold Freeman

August 8, 2011

Back in the 1960s, when what is now the nation of Eritrea was still part of Ethiopia, a student from a village out in the Eritrean countryside lived with three Peace Corps Volunteers in what might be called the county-seat town, Mendefera. That was so he could attend the secondary school there, which was the only one in the region.

The student, Yemane [say "Ye-mah-nay"], was fortunate to get to do this, because at that time only a very small fraction of Ethiopians could read and write.

Eventually Yemane invited the volunteers, all of whom taught at his school, to visit his village so they could see his home and so his mother and little brothers could meet the people with whom he lived.

The visitors rode their bikes 10 or 12 miles along a narrow, paved highway and then turned off onto a dirt road that gave way to what was basically a bumpy path with lots of rocks alongside. Two or three miles of that took them to the village and to Yemane's family's one-room house. It had a dirt floor, and for seating there was a hard-packed earthen bench along an inside wall.

In the middle of the floor was a small stove on which Yemane's mother, squatting, did the cooking. She had prepared a fine meal—one rare for ordinary folks because it included stewed chicken and boiled eggs. Such a feast was usually reserved for holidays.

The Americans were introduced to other residents of the village, were treated like honored guests, and were well fed. Then, when it came time for them to leave, Yemane's mother presented them with eggs as a parting gift. The Peace Corps volunteers hesitated, knowing that she and her younger sons needed the eggs much more than they did.

However, the visitors also were aware of the Ethiopian and Eritrean tradition of hospitality and generosity, and they could not offend their hostess by simply declining this gift. Thinking that they were being both truthful and clever, they explained that because the road was so bumpy, the bouncing bicycles would break the eggs and they would be wasted.

Yemane's mother accepted this line of reasoning, and the Peace Corps volunteers were relieved until she said, "Then you must take the chicken." And that's what they did.

JOURNEY TO ETHIOPIA: 1962-1964

Isaac Joseph, My Good Friend

Isaac Joseph, a fellow teacher, became my closest Eritrean friend. His rounded face and turned up nose reminded some people of a sculpture that is believed to be of the Greek philosopher, Socrates, and Isaac liked being associated with another philosopher like himself. He had a far-reaching curiosity, and he was non-judgmental about most of the topics he explored. We remained friends for half a century, from September 1962 until his death on July 20, 2012. Because of our friendship, stories about Isaac appear throughout this book.

I first noticed Isaac immediately after the opening day of school in September 1962. In our first meeting with teachers, he asked, "Why do the Red Indians have no beards?" The question was typical of Isaac's inquiring mind.

Isaac taught 5th and 6th grade English and social studies, and I regret that I never saw him or any of my other colleagues when they were teaching. I was too busy in my own classrooms, and it probably would have been awkward, but I wish I had seen them teaching. I might have become a better teacher if I had seen how my colleagues did it.

Eritreans and Ethiopians have their own distinct style of music. Soon after we had settled into the boys' house, I bought a small record player in Asmara. It operated on the town's electric current, so we used it only when the Adi Ugri generator was running, from 4:00 p.m. to 7:00 a.m. The first record I bought was "Through Children's Eyes," a collection of songs for kids recorded by the Limelighters in 1962. Some of the Limelighter songs were "500 Miles Away from Home," "Michael Row the Boat Ashore," and "Amen," and Isaac liked the songs.

I also bought a record of classical music by J.S. Bach, and I was eager to play it for Isaac. When I played the Bach record, Isaac said, "Please, Mr. Nyle, please turn it off. It hurts my ears!"

Eritrean music follows a single melody line, and harmony must sound to Eritreans like there is more than one song playing at once. I don't remember hearing musical harmony in Eritrea unless it was foreign music, usually performed by foreigners.

Isaac led a scout group that included girls as well as boys. His scout leader's uniform was a khaki shirt and shorts with a scouts emblem on the shirt. He even had a pointed forest ranger hat, and a neckerchief. One Sunday afternoon, I went on a scout hike with Isaac and his scouts.

We set out at a fast pace through the countryside, following well-worn paths that led between fields from village to village. I was only twenty-three years old, but I felt like an old man compared to the young Eritrean boys and girls. One of the boys irreverently called me "Mr. Tumtumo," comparing me to a dish of a bland Eritrean bean mash. He was at least partly right.

We hiked past a grain field that was being guarded by a country girl armed with the kind of sling that David used to kill Goliath in that Bible story. The girl's sling was made of braided yarn about six feet long, bent in half in the middle. At the bend, there was a small pocket for a stone. The girl put a finger through a loop in the cord, and she gripped the straight end of the cord in the same hand.

She loaded a stone into the sling's pocket and whirled the sling overhead while trilling loudly in a high-pitched voice. She took two long, leaping steps toward the field while whirling the sling overhead, and fired a shot through the tall stalks of grain. The stone went crackling through the grain like a bullet, but it would have been only by chance if it had hit a bird. She just wanted to scare away the marauding birds.

Seeing the girl throw a stone with her sling helped me understand how David could bring down that giant, Goliath, with a stone from his sling. The stone must have hit Goliath's head like a bullet from a high caliber pistol.

Isaac and I were having tea in a shop in Adi Ugri one day when an oddly dressed man walked in. His clothing was colorful and dramatic, and he wore a dark turban around his head. The man came in to buy tea, but the tea shop owner said, "The seats in this place are reserved for their owners."

It was a politically phrased threat, and the man left. Isaac told me what the man had said. He explained, "That man was a spy. I feel sure of it." Isaac may have been right.

After I left Ethiopia in 1964, Isaac and I remained friends. We wrote letters, but we only very rarely spoke on the phone because international calls were so expensive back then. I called him from Wisconsin to ask for the recipe for *ful*, the breakfast bean mash. The call cost $30 U.S. equal to about $80 in our dollars now.

JOURNEY TO ETHIOPIA: 1962-1964

Another time, I was longing for spicy Ethiopian food but I had no beri-beri, the Ethiopian hot pepper and spice mixture. I wrote to Isaac and asked if he would mail some beri-beri to me. I expected him to send a small sample, maybe one or two cups of it. A month or so later, a large package came in the mail. The package was the size of a five-pound bag of sugar, and it weighed over two pounds. Inside the package was a plastic bag of beri-beri seasoning. The package was wrapped in coarse grey paper, taped shut, and tied with strings. Isaac obviously thought I would be cooking *zigini* often and making it very hot with beri-beri. I put the beri-beri in jars and kept the jars in the freezer to preserve the flavor, and I used it for years. I still have some of that ancient beri-beri in my freezer in 2024.

In 1987, Isaac was put in prison in Eritrea because he had written political pamphlets and books in Tigrinya. I assume his writings were thoughtful examinations of Eritrean and Ethiopian political issues and the history behind them. The pamphlets had not gotten him into trouble under Haile Selassie, but the Leftists of the Derg put him in prison and accused Isaac of spying because of the letters he and I had written to each other.

The Derg was a Marxist-Leninist movement within the Ethiopian army that carried out radical steps intended to change the basic character of Ethiopian government and society.

In one of his letters, Isaac told me it was cold in the prison during the Eritrean nights. To keep him warm at night, I sent him a space-age plastic blanket. It was made of something called "Mylar" that was plastic on one side and as shiny as a mirror on the other side. The whole blanket folded into a 4" by 4" packet less than half an inch thick. Isaac could wrap himself in the Mylar blanket with the shiny side in, and the shiny surface reflected his body heat back to him and kept him warm. The packet and blanket somehow made it through customs and prison security to Isaac, a modern miracle. Isaac was released from prison in January 1990 after three years.

Isaac and I remained in contact for the rest of his life. In 1994 I returned to Eritrea for my only visit after leaving in 1964. Isaac was my guide and companion for that trip. One day we drove past what I would call a soccer stadium. I reminded Isaac that Americans call the game soccer, not football, but we have a game we call football.

Isaac thought a moment and said, "Yes! I have seen American football! They just put their hands on the ball and they fight each other, struggling and fighting like animals!"

Isaac stayed with me and my family in Indianapolis a few years later when he was in the States as a representative of the Eritrean Orthodox Church.

I was in Kenya in June 2012, and I called Isaac in Eritrea from there. He had been having a health issue, and he died a few weeks later. Rest in peace, my good, thoughtful friend.

I used some of Isaac's beri-beri and my own recipes for injera and zigini to cook enough for fifty people at the International Festival at Brookfield Academy in Wisconsin. I later cooked the same food on a smaller scale for the teachers at Wichita Collegiate School and at Sycamore School in Indianapolis.

Leaving Eritrea

"Oh, the days dwindle down to a precious few . . ."

(From "September Song" by Anderson Maxwell, Weill Kurt)

Near the end of the school year in 1964, we Ethiopia Peace Corps teachers were completing our two-year commitment and were excited to be leaving. We thought it would be wonderful to leave Ethiopia and start for home. We didn't realize how deeply our time there had affected us.

Gloria Somple and John Rude flew directly from Asmara to the States, but I wanted to take a longer route in Ethiopia and in Europe.

On July 3, 1964, the Peace Corps' Volkswagen pickup truck came to Adi Ugri to pick me up with my luggage. I had been longing to leave Ethiopia and return to the States, but when the Peace Corps truck was climbing up the last hill north of Adi Ugri, I leaned out the window and looked back at the little city that had been my home for two years. I cried when I realized how much I loved Adi Ugri. We rounded a bend, and there was nothing to do but look forward.

The next night, July 4 fireworks at Kagnew Station punctuated the end of my Eritrea years. To me, the fireworks were a celebration of my return to the United States.

JOURNEY TO ETHIOPIA: 1962-1964

The sixty Eritrea volunteers could travel on our own to Addis Ababa and fly out of the country from there, or we could wait in Eritrea and meet the outbound jet at the Asmara airport for the flight to Athens. I wanted to see more of Ethiopia, so I bought a ticket for the three-day bus trip to Addis Ababa. The bus made overnight stops at Mekele and Dessie in Ethiopia, and reached Addis Ababa on the third day.

After two days in Addis Ababa, I boarded a jet for the outbound flight. The 90-minute flight from Addis Ababa to Asmara reversed the trip that had taken three days by bus. The other Eritrea volunteers boarded the Boeing 707 at Asmara, and we were off to Athens.

The Journey Home

Before I set off for Europe, I bought a copy of "Europe on $5 Dollars a Day" to supplement my early National Geographic education. The book was first published for civilians in 1957, and in 1964 you could still travel in Europe for about $5 per day. It now costs $79 to $100 a day to travel in Europe if you are careful. Just think of it as $10 an hour.

On the 1962 trip to Ethiopia, we were in Athens only one day, so in 1964 I arranged to spend more time there, reliving the *National Geographic* pictures I had gazed at as a boy in Ohio. The Acropolis and the Parthenon were still in Athens, and they were as stunning as they had seemed in *National Geographic* pictures. I hiked around ancient ruins and ate in Greek restaurants and saw the "Son and Lumiere" – Sound and Light – program at the brightly lighted Parthenon.

At dusk, drivers in Athens didn't immediately turn on their headlights. They zoomed along in the lowering darkness and turned on their lights only when they could see that other cars were approaching. The drivers may have thought they were saving electricity, or maybe they were trying to extend the life of their headlights.

I was the victim of a small international incident in Athens. I took a table at an outdoor restaurant and ordered lunch. I waited a very long time, and no lunch came. I finally got up and walked away. Soon a waiter came out yelling angrily to me. He must have had my long-delayed lunch. I didn't care. I bought a sandwich some other place, not knowing if I was a victim of anti-American prejudice.

I took a one-day cruise to islands in the Aegean Sea and saw brilliant white stone shores and the ruins of Greek temples. *National Geographic* had not deceived me.

On the bus trip to Corinth, Greece, the bus crossed the Corinth Canal, a 4-mile passage carved through towering cliffs to avoid a 430-mile trip around the Peloponnesian Peninsula. A painting in a 1944 *National Geographic* had shown men hauling ships on rollers across the isthmus in ancient times, centuries before the Corinth Canal was built.

When I left Athens, I boarded a boat at the nearby Greek port of Piraeus and set sail for Italy. It was early evening when the boat passed through the towering walls of the Corinth Canal, so this time I saw it from sea level. The canal had been envisioned in ancient times, but it wasn't created until 1893. The canal is too narrow for large, ocean-going ships, but the ferry from Greece to Italy was small enough to squeeze through.

The boat ticket to Italy included a hammock where I could try to sleep through the overnight trip in an interior room with other men in hammocks. The Adriatic Sea was cold, even in July, so shelter from the cold wind was welcome. The sea was rough, and we rocked in our hammocks through waves like those that drove the Apostle Paul's ship against a rocky shore.

At Brindisi in southern Italy, I bought a third-class ticket for a train to Naples, and I got what I paid for. My seat was a wooden bench. I was young, and I slept fairly well on that bench.

In 1964, the train from Brindisi to Naples took ten hours. Trains today make the Brindisi to Naples trip in less than six hours.

The train left Brindisi in the evening, and the train stopped early in the morning somewhere in southern Italy. A man walked along the station platform yelling, "Café! Café caldo!" I had learned enough Italian in Eritrea to know he was selling hot coffee. I bought a steaming cup of coffee and a sweet roll, and I was revived.

On a street in Naples, a woman carrying a baby came up to me and asked for money and I gave her some. Begging was common in Africa, but I was shocked to see a beggar in Europe.

JOURNEY TO ETHIOPIA: 1962-1964

At Naples, I found a cheap hotel and bought a ticket for the bus ride to the nearby ruins of Pompeii. That city had been buried under ash when Mount Vesuvius erupted in 79 AD. In 1964 Pompeii was being uncovered. Some of the cobblestone streets had been cleared, and I admired beautiful frescoes painted on interior walls. I was again walking through a *National Geographic* article.

After Naples, I spent four nights in Rome and met up with other Ethiopia Peace Corps people, including John Rex, a musician. He invited some of us to see the opera "Aida" at the ancient Baths of Caracalla one steamy night. At the opening of the "Triumphal March," a team of four horses pulled a Roman chariot from the back of the stage and thundered forward toward the audience. People in front screamed, and the horses reared up and halted at the edge of the orchestra pit. The rest of the Triumphal March was mild in comparison.

At the Colosseum in Rome, I met a young Catholic priest who spoke to me in French. We chatted in my beginner's French and he asked, "*Croyez-vous que Jesus Christos ete le fis de l'eternelle?*" (Do you believe that Jesus Christ was the Son of the Eternal God?) I replied, *"Oui."* I doubt that I tried to say much more because my French was so poor, but I was pleased to find that I could share the faith at the Colosseum, where so many Christian martyrs had died.

On a less spiritual note, I looked out of my hotel window one morning across an alley where another hotel glowed in the early morning sun. A woman who was in her fifties was standing at an open window, and she was as naked as the day she was born. That was a quick lesson on the effects of aging, but I wasn't ready to know so much right then.

From Rome I took a train north, hoping for cooler weather. I didn't even get off the train at Florence because the day was so hot, and I still haven't seen Florence. I went on to see the canals in Venice and saw the plaza at the Basilica de Saint Marco, which is sinking slowly into the sea.

The train went through Innsbruck, Austria and the cool mountain air was its own reward. The mountain scene at Innsbruck would have reminded me of Heidi and her grandfather if I had read the book.

My cousin, Dr. Jon Kardatzke, was "suffering" through his military duty as an Army doctor at Oberammergau. No one ever suffered in a more beautiful place. The town was immaculately clean, and trout swam in cold streams beside flower-lined streets. It was not a year for the Oberammergau passion play, so the town was quiet.

Jon and his wife Lorna took me to see a medieval castle and a German beer garden. At the beer garden, a brass quartet played German marching songs and a stocky man in leather shorts threw a broomstick over one shoulder and goose-stepped across the stage. It might have been an illegal act, since World War Two had ended less than twenty year earlier, and memories of Nazi times still hung in the air. I don't remember roaring applause that evening in 1964.

Munich was so crowded that most of the hotels were fully booked. I met an American tourist, and he offered to share his tiny room in a modest hotel. He took the bed, and I slept on a little couch. As we talked, I learned the man was grieving the fact that his girlfriend had had an abortion. He was wrenched with grief and guilt, and the revelry of Munich only heightened his pain. I knew of only one other abortion at that time. I hope I comforted the man by listening to him in his grief.

From Oberammergau, a train took me to Lucerne, Switzerland, where I intercepted a group of Anderson College students who were touring Europe with Professor Tom Pappas. The main thing I learned from Dr. Pappas was how to eat cheese fondue. We speared little cubes of bread on fondue forks and plunged the bread into a pot of hot, melted cheese. It was the wrong time of year for hot cheese, but it added to my life as a world traveler. I became so European that I even have a fondue pot and a hot plate for it… somewhere.

The next stop was Geneva, Switzerland, where I spent a Sunday afternoon walking along the southern shore of Lake Geneva. My only memory of that day was a plume of water rising above a fountain in the lake. The history of Geneva was lost on me. I was thinking of Paris.

The night train to Paris must have been comfortable. I slept until the train slowed to a crawl and stopped at the Gare du Lyon, one of the main train stations in Paris. In the station, I saw a bar full of businessmen having beer and small cakes for breakfast. They evidently were able to work after drinking, and probably were only a little "under the influence" when they reached their offices or stores. I stuck with café au lait and pastries to start my day.

JOURNEY TO ETHIOPIA: 1962-1964

The slow trip from Geneva to Paris took all night in 1964. Regular trains do it in five and a half hours now. On the TGV, the "train de grande vitesse" – the "train of great speed," the trip now takes about three hours.

In Paris, I found a youth hostel for cheap lodging, though at twenty-four I was at least a little over the usual age for lodgers there. The hostel was like a large barracks, and it was managed by two caretakers. I left my luggage with the caretakers and went off to explore the fabled city. I had read about Paris in history books and in my French textbook, and I was ready for the real thing. I met a man about my age, and we set off on foot to find the most famous places we could think of. He had a map, and it looked as though we could cut through a residential neighborhood to the Eifel Tower.

While we were studying the map, a dapper gentleman in a beret came along and asked, *"Vous cherchez quelque chose?"* (You are looking for something?)

We three looked over the map together, and my new friend spoke French with the gentleman. I can't prove it, but I feel sure the man was Piaget, the child psychologist. He was teaching at the University of Paris in 1964, so it *must* have been him.

The Paris subway system, the Metro, is one of the wonders of the modern world. I bought a map of the Metro and reliably surfaced near many of the most famous sites.

I went to the Paris flea market one afternoon, and at a small concession stand, sausages on buns (like hot dogs) were being sold by a surly woman. I got in line behind two Frenchmen, and the first man stepped to the window. The man ordered sausage on bun, and the woman asked, *"Volez-vous de la mutard?"* (Do you want mustard?)

The man stood there, speechless. The woman raised her voice, fairly yelling, *"Voulez-vous de la mutard?"*

"Oui!" the man stammered and received his sausage.

The next man went to the window and ordered a sausage. Again, the woman asked, *"Voulez-vous de la mutard?"*

As before, this man stood in a daze until she yelled, *"VOULEZ-VOUS DE LA MUTARD?"*

"Oui!" the man replied meekly, got his sausage with mustard, and went away.

It was my turn. I had learned a lesson, and I was ready. I asked for sausage on a bun, and the woman asked, *"Voulez-vous de la mutard?"*

"Oui, Madame!" I said confidently in my best Parisian French with mustard.

The woman wasn't impressed, but I did get a sausage on a bun with mustard, and the woman didn't yell at me. It was one of my finer linguistic moments.

I went to the art museum called the Louvre and looked for the most famous things I had heard of. Venus de Milo was there, and I made sure not to stand and stare too long.

Another incident from Paris is worth reporting. I was in front of the historic Crillon Hotel when I saw Don Kent, the man who had been in charge of the United States Information Service in Asmara. At the moment I saw him, I confused him with Clark Kent, the mild-mannered newspaper reporter who could turn into Superman. To get Don Kent's attention, I called out, "Mr. Clark!"

This may not have been the first time he was mistaken for Superman. He turned and recognized me as a Peace Corps volunteer from Eritrea. He invited me into the Crillon for refreshments, and we talked of Ethiopia. As we were leaving, Henry Cabot Lodge came down a flight of stairs into the lobby. Don Kent greeted him. "Good evening, Mr. Ambassador."

Lodge returned the greeting. I stood in awe. Needless to say, Lodge didn't recognize me and didn't greet me by name.

Until June 1964, Lodge had been the American Ambassador to South Vietnam. The war in Vietnam began to heat up later that summer due to the Bay of Tonkin incident.

When I had seen as much as I could in Paris, I caught a train to Brussels, Belgium. On the train, I sat across the aisle from two British ladies, one of whom had a little dog on her lap. The ladies talked at length about the virtues of dogs—all dogs, not just the one with them. They talked of the intelligence of dogs and their capacity for sympathy and their ability to read the minds of their masters. This seemed a little overdone, and it gave me the impression that British people dote on their dogs a bit too much. I may have been wrong. It was just a first impression.

JOURNEY TO ETHIOPIA: 1962-1964

Brussels was a friendly city where the past hung heavy in the air. I walked around a square lined with buildings that may have been there when Columbus sailed the ocean blue, but he didn't sail from Brussels or anyplace nearby. The food was especially good in Brussels.

My next stop was at Amsterdam, in the Netherlands. I found a cheap hotel a few blocks from the train station, and that evening I talked with two men in a bar. One of them said that religion is really the basis for understanding life. The other man and I nodded in agreement. It was good to know that religion and God could be present in a bar.

The next day was Sunday, and the morning streets were nearly empty. I headed for the train station to check the schedules and scampered across an intersection just in time to avoid being hit by a car that was speeding toward me. I heard screeching tires, a thump, and a crash, and I looked back and saw a man fly up over the top of the car. He landed in the street, bounced, and skidded to a stop in the street. The motorcycle he had been riding spun away and stopped down the street. A small crowd gathered around the unconscious motorcyclist. An ambulance came, and it seemed likely the man would die. I couldn't do anything helpful, so I went to the station and bought a train ticket.

From Amsterdam I took a train to a seaside dock to get on a boat to England. It was a short daytime ferry trip, and the boat was crowded, so I sat down at the side of an outdoor walkway and leaned against a wall. Beside me was an American high school teacher who may have been in his forties. The teacher didn't say what he taught; his main interest was American cars, and he talked about cars. Talking of one of his favorite cars he said, "If you have a car like that, you're really living."

I had been in Africa for two years, and I had rarely driven a car in that time. After what I had seen in Africa, the man's love of cars seemed shallow and immature, but I politely kept my mouth shut. Before long, back in America, I soon had a similar interest in cars and their ability to elevate life.

In London, I found a cheap hotel near a train station. The hotel felt like one from the 1890s: cold, dark, with a slightly musty smell, but it served as my home base while I looked for the places I had heard of. As in Paris, *Europe on Five Dollars a Day* was my guide, and I used the "tube" (what we would call a subway) to get around. The tube took me all over

London, and I surfaced like a prairie dog in several places. At every stop I found myself at a place I had heard of.

In no particular order, I saw the dazzling lights of Piccadilly Circus, the grim walls of the Tower of London, the changing of the guard at Buckingham Palace, Tower Bridge, Big Ben clock, Parliament building, the front of British Museum, and a church designed by the famous architect, Christopher Wren.

One place I surfaced was a few blocks from Downing Street which I knew is the home of the Prime Minister. I was able to walk right up to the Prime Minister's door to take a picture. A courier arrived on a small motorcycle and went in with a message, and another person came out. I was there several minutes, but no one invited me in.

When I left London, a bus took me west to Birkenhead, a city on the River Mersey on the west side of England. Liverpool, home of the Beatles, was across the river. I was there to see John and Maisie Larmour, my older brother's in-laws. I went with their son to buy a carryout evening meal of fish and "chips," and I felt almost like a native. I was happy that I could speak a dialect of their language.

John Larmour advised me to fly from England to Ireland because the Irish Sea would be rough and cold. I took his advice and bought a ticket for the short flight, and I found a room for the night in in a private home in Dublin, Ireland. My bed that night was a couch that was so short that I had to sleep with my knees drawn up. That was to be my last night in Europe for several years.

Last Leg of the Trip Home

On the last day of the long journey, I picked up my heavy suitcase and caught a bus from Dublin across Ireland toward the international airport at Shannon, Ireland. The bus jiggled along through a green countryside that seemed soggy from frequent rain. At a rural intersection, the conductor told me the bus didn't go any closer to Shannon and would be going off in different direction. I could see the airport, so I picked up my suitcase, got off the bus, and started walking. A kind-hearted Irishman in a pickup truck offered me a ride. I threw my suitcase in the back of his truck, and he delivered me to the airport.

JOURNEY TO ETHIOPIA: 1962-1964

The plane took off from Shannon in early afternoon with the sun high overhead. Instead of the day speeding by as it had on the eastbound Atlantic crossing in 1962, the sun nearly stood still on this westbound flight. Flying west at 600 miles per hour, the plane flew toward the slowly lowering sun. The sun was still high in the sky in late afternoon when the plane landed at Boston. The final flight of the journey was from Boston to Chicago's O'Hare Field, and I was soon on a bus to downtown Chicago. My older brother, Merl, picked me up, and the next afternoon we drove to Elmore, Ohio, where my journey to Ethiopia had begun.

Some things in the States were familiar, but in a strange new way. I was no longer the 22-year-old who had left two years earlier. I wasn't really a world traveler, but I had seen a lot in two years. The strangeness of my own country began to settle on me. I was having "reverse culture shock," the feeling that your own country seems lonely and strange. I hadn't heard of reverse culture shock, and I was blind-sided by it, but if I had known the term and its meaning, I still might have had the emotional upheaval I felt in my first few months back in the States.

At home near Elmore, Ohio that first night, I lay down in the bed where I had slept the night before the flight to New York two years earlier. It was good to be at home with images and memories swirling through my mind. I could think back to where I had been; I couldn't envision what was still to come for me or for the places I had seen.

We shall not cease from exploration,
And the end of all our exploring
Will be to arrive where we started,
And know the place for the first time.
Through the unknown, unremembered gate
When the last of earth left to discover
Is that which was the beginning.
At the source of the longest river,
The voice of the hidden waterfall

T.S. Eliot, from "Little Gidding," 1942

APPENDIX

ROADS AND VILLAGES OF ERITREA

SOME OF MY MOST MEMORABLE experiences in Eritrea were visits to nearby villages in the highlands and in the more remote lowlands to the west. Roads lead out of Asmara in all four directions. One road goes north and makes an arc westward through Keren, Agordat, Barentu, and Tessenei in Eritrea. That road continues on to Kassala in Sudan. A smaller road goes north from Keren to Afabet and Nakfa, towns that were centers of the Eritrean Liberation Front during the Eritrean war in the 1990s. To the northeast, the road to Massawa twists and turns on a scenic route down the mountains. It passes through Nefasit, Ghinda, and Dogali and ends in sand flats near Massawa.

Two roads lead south out of Asmara. The easterly of those two roads goes through Dekemhare, Adi Keyh, and Senafe before entering Ethiopia. The other road to the south passes through Debarwa, Teraemni, Mendefera (Adi Ugri), and Adi Quala and goes on to Adwa in Ethiopia. The two southerly roads meet before they go to Mekele, the capital of Tigray Province in northern Ethiopia. Besides these main roads, there are many gravel tracks, trails, and footpaths in Eritrea, and there probably are far more paved roads now.

Just west of the St. George School was the village of Barack, bearing the name of the future American president. Adi Mengonti was northwest of

Adi Ugri, and Kodofelassie was to the southeast. Less than a mile south of the school a little village called Ziban Una shimmered in the afternoon sun. Each village seemed to have stories and mysteries of its own.

I traveled as many of these roads as I could. I wish I could have seen more.

Moments of My Return

I had flown into Chicago from Europe, and I spent that first night at the home of my older brother. The next day, we drove to Ohio and surprised my sister Sharon by intercepting her on her way to her evening job at a restaurant. In the excitement of our seeing each other, her car was still in gear when we jumped out to hug. Sharon's arm was momentarily pinned between the two open car doors, but she slipped away uninjured.

My mother then took me to the Sun Oil refinery in Toledo and asked the guard at the gate to call my dad from his work. He came out and met us in the parking lot. In his joy and surprise, he said, "Well! There's the boy!" It was like the father's joy when the Prodigal Son returned.

Gloria Olive Saves My Mathematics Life

This story tells how I became a math teacher in spite of my weak start in math, and it describes a daring act by my college math professor, Gloria Olive.

I went to college by accident in September 1957, not having planned on college during my high school years. In the fall semester 1958, I signed up for algebra and analytical geometry, a course that any self-respecting math student would have taken in high school. The course was challenging, but I found I could do it. Miss Olive's teaching was clear, and it was obvious that she especially liked talented math students. I became one of Miss Olive's fair-haired boys. I started strong, and I went into the final exam riding the possibility of earning an A, a new experience in my checkered school life.

That's when the trouble began. When Miss Olive handed out the exam papers, I stared at the test in disbelief. I could see the problems I was to solve, but I didn't understand a thing. I began whacking away at answers, uncertain of most of them. When the exam period ended, I handed in my work and left for my rooming house across the street from Old Main. Having flunked such an important exam, I thought my college career was over.

Suddenly the pay phone rang in the hallway outside my room.

"Hello?" I answered cautiously.

The voice at the other end was unmistakable. It was Gloria Olive. "I would like to speak with Nyle Kardatzke," she said in her precise, deliberate way.

"This is Nyle," I said shaking in fear.

"Mister Kardatzke!" Miss Olive began. "This is Miss Olive. I have graded your exam, and I don't accept it! Come to my office right now."

Going to her office after failing the exam seemed like facing death. I paused for a moment to contemplate death and said, "Oh, okay. I'll be right there."

"Have a seat," she said when I walked in, and she directed me to the end of a long table. She walked over and slapped an exam on the table in front of me.

"I want you to take the exam again. The one you handed in did not look like your work," she said.

I looked at the exam. It was the same exam, but this time, the scales fell from my eyes. I knew everything! I began solving equations and performing all the required mathematical operations with blazing speed. I finished quickly and handed in my exam feeling confident, even exultant.

When the semester grades were released, I had an A on the exam and an A in the course. At the first class meeting in January, Miss Olive gave me a knowing smile as she handed me my exam bluebook. My future was set. I became a math major. Miss Olive had taken a bold step and had saved my academic life, a power play that most professors wouldn't have taken. She put me back on track and "that has made all the difference."

> *Two roads diverged in a wood, and I—*
> *I took the one less traveled by,*
> *And that has made all the difference.*
>
> *(From "The Road Not Taken" by Robert Frost)*

JOURNEY TO ETHIOPIA: 1962-1964

Eaten by a Crocodile

In spring 1966, I was living in Indiana. I was shocked when I read a short article in Newsweek Magazine about a Peace Corps teacher, Bill Olson, who had been killed by a crocodile in Ethiopia. I later learned Bill had been teaching science in Adi Ugri, as I had. He had been living in the same house where I had lived, and Yemane Russom had been his houseboy. Yemane later met Bill Olson's family in Wisconsin. What follows are excerpts from a Peace Corps publication about the tragedy.

"Remembering Gambela" by Steve Buff (Ethiopia 1964–66) – This article was written following the publication in PeaceCorpsWriters.org, November, 2000 of "A Letter from Ethiopia" by Kathleen Coskran, who told of the tragic death of PCV William Olson, which she witnessed.

During our spring vacation in 1966, close to our scheduled departure from Ethiopia, my wife-to-be, Evelyn Ashkenaze, and I flew to Gambela to see a very different Ethiopia from the one we knew in Shoa province. This was not the Ethiopia of cool highlands and white flowing traditional dress, but Nilotic Africa, in the blazing southwestern lowlands near the Sudanese border. The people were semi-nomadic, extremely tall and blue-black; the villagers nearby were barely clothed in the heat and the women adorned with elaborate wide, high necklaces. This was much closer to our childhood National Geographic images of Africa than any place we'd seen before in Ethiopia.

We spent a few days trekking around the area, seeing the sights, and meeting the local people, known to us then as the Anuak and Nuer. One afternoon, as [we] were enjoying ourselves paddling around the river in a dugout canoe, we became aware of a group of folks swimming in the river.

We then heard alarmed shouts coming from the group and immediately paddled toward the PCVs, who were across the river and downstream from us. They yelled that one of their companions, whom we later learned was William Olson, had just disappeared while swimming off a sandbar in the middle of the river. It soon appeared likely that he had been pulled down by a crocodile. He never resurfaced.

Villagers gathered at the riverbank and there was much agitation and discussion. They were joined by an American army colonel named Dow who was on safari with a Swiss guide, Karl Luthy. They were traveling with powerful rifles intended for big game. We learned from Luthy and from several other people that this group of PCVs (or at least some members of the group) had been warned repeatedly not to go into the river that a large crocodile lived in a bank nearby and had "taken" a woman only recently. Luthy makes this clear in his account of the tragedy, which appears in the book Eyelids of Morning.

[We] paddled back and forth along the river until dusk searching for any sign of the crocodile or Bill Olson. In the evening, many groups, including Dow and Luthy, continued searching. George, his cousin, Evelyn and I scanned the river and its banks with searchlights from George's Jeep. There was no sign of the crocodile.

The search resumed early the next morning. Before long, the crocodile surfaced and, after several attempts, it was killed by Colonel Dow. (We still have one of the shells.) The thing was so huge and heavy that it was a struggle for several men to pull it through shallow water and onto a sandy low part of shore. Townspeople were rejoicing. It was a victory, after all, over a dragon, an historic enemy of the Anuak and Nuer, a monster whose kind had pulled down and fed on children and adults on river shores for as long as anyone could remember.

There it lay, facing the river, fluid dribbling out of its closed jaws, broad, tall, enormous, a nightmarish alien species, more like a dinosaur than anything else. Luthy was anxious to cut open the crocodile's belly. Evelyn stepped a few feet away and turned in the opposite direction. Luthy, with considerable insensitivity, said, "Let's see what's in here" and cut the crocodile open with a large hunter's knife. Gelatinous stuff billowed out of its mouth. There was no longer any doubt about Olson's end.

I know of no other Peace Corps volunteer who met such a tragic end. Rest in peace, Bill Olson.

www.ingramcontent.com/pod-product-compliance
Lightning Source LLC
Chambersburg PA
CBHW072156070526
44585CB00015B/1163